Grandmother
Had No Name

Grandmother

Had No Name

by ALICE MURONG PU LIN

CHINA
BOOKS
& Periodicals, Inc.

Cover design by Robbin L. Henderson

©1988 by Alice P. Lin

All Rights reserved. No part of this book may be used or
reproduced in any manner whatsoever without permission
in writing from the publisher. Address inquiries to China
Books, 2929 24th Street, San Francisco, CA 94110

ISBN 0-8351-2045-7 (casebound)

ISBN 0-8351-2034-1 (paperback)

Printed in the United States of America by 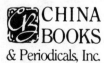 CHINA
BOOKS
& Periodicals, Inc.

Dedicated to my parents—
General and Mrs. Lianshao Pu

Contents

PART ONE

The Chinese Family Between Tradition and Modernity

PART TWO

Between East and West — Taiwan and America

Acknowledgements

I have been in the United States for more than half my lifetime. In many ways, I consider myself an American-Chinese, more American than Chinese as the years go by. Yet my Chinese blood runs deep, my ties with Chinese culture remain strong. On the way to becoming Western-ized, I have relinquished but have also retained some of my old values and beliefs. I have long been part of both the Eastern and Western worlds, and for both I have the deepest affection.

My sincere thanks to Malcolm Willison for his thoughtful and meticulous reading of my first draft. Above all, I am grateful to my family—my husband, Nan, and my two sons, Clement Ho and Michael Ping—for their moral support.

Foreword: To My Chinese Sisters

It was one summer evening in 1982 that I knew I had to write to you. I was visiting my great aunt in her tiny but well-kept apartment in Wuhan, China, near where I was teaching at a summer institute. I had not met Great Aunt Li before this trip, nor had I even known of her existence during the thirty-three years of my living abroad. Here I was, sipping hot, fragrant jasmine tea and listening to her account of the intervening years. Great Aunt Li, sister-in-law to my maternal grandmother, a petite woman, standing four feet eleven in her bound, cloth-clad feet, was in her late eighties at that time. She was a mesmerizing woman; energy seemed to flow from her tiny torso to me.

Great Aunt Li had had no formal education at all. Under the old social structure women did not enjoy the privilege of public education, which was reserved for just the sons of better families. But somehow she managed to learn to read on her own, and soon devoured all the books in the house, which were supposed to be reserved for men. Her reading was a secret, especially her interest in romantic novels. This secret passion she kept alive even during the Cultural Revolution of the 1960s. Great Aunt Li hid away all the novels of the house in her attic. She recounted her "undercover activities" with a gleam: "I kept them well hidden so no one ever found me reading."

It hit me like a thunderbolt. Keep your secret so no one will know; survive by keeping your thoughts from men. Keep silent so the deceit can go on. We were women from two different generations and two different cultures, yet we shared the same pain and dilemma in different spheres of our lives. The choice of silence is no more hers than mine. We have carried that conditioned response into the outside world—a man's world—and we have yet to emerge as a group with faith in ourselves and others. The war between men and women still wages on.

That summer, I would be moved again and again by what I saw and heard. I spoke to my students in the program, some of them well-established women holding high positions in the People's Republic of China, and found a different and yet a similar perspective on womanhood. I left China to go to Hong Kong and discovered clear evidence of the same struggle, the struggle for independence and a more harmonious relationship with men. I visited Taiwan and South Korea and found the common ties of womanhood there as well. I asked questions and was asked many in return.

Then I returned to the United States. For a long time afterward I felt like a kite with a broken string, the string that connects me with my Chinese sisters and with other Asian women. I started having dreams. In my dreams I saw faces of different Asian women, some familiar, some not, speaking to me. I heard the silent prayers of many women, from thousands of years past. I saw the joyless state of married women, subjugating their entire identities to their new families and to the men they served. I saw them standing in courtyards trying to run their households while the men were out seeking their separate enjoyment. I saw them most clearly in modern attire, speaking of equality for women while continuing with the traditional roles at home.

I realized even in my own dreams that I was one of them. I am just as culturally conditioned as they are. I had become more acutely aware of their joys and pains, for I shared them, as I share them with my Western sisters. Womanhood knows no national or ethnic boundaries. Our shared secrets bridge the centuries and continents.

For the past few years, following my first return to China since 1949, I have thought about my Chinese sisters. I have thought about the long road we have traveled together, how far we have come yet how much we still lag behind in our quest for recognition and equality. I have thought how typical it was for Great Aunt Li not to complain, for most of us Chinese women have not. We have tolerated much.

Returning from my 1982 trip to China, there was little doubt in my mind that optimism was in the air. Women in my classes spoke not of women's issues, but of issues concerning all people. The Chinese National Organization for Women, with its headquarters in Beijing and affiliates in the provinces, had been devoting all its attention to social welfare programs throughout China. The 1950 Marriage Law of the new People's Republic of China had given women a legal foundation for achieving dignity and equality in marriage, divorce, and property settlements. Women had equal rights to education, and women had been moving steadily into managerial and administrative positions. The old structure of male domination seemed to have faded into the past.

In the summer of 1985, three years after the beginning of China's major push for a one-child family planning policy, I went back to China with a New York State delegation of academicians and government officials. I now began to see the old attitude, creeping back in—the *only* child had better be a *male* child. Contradictory reports about female infanticide were often denied by public officials, but there was strong evidence that enforcement of the one-child per couple policy was encouraging the reemergence of the ancient preference for male offspring, especially in the countryside. In the old China, sons were needed to carry on the family name, to till the fields, to provide support in your old age.

The national government did step in to prosecute known cases of female infanticide and to institute an educational campaign to promote the value of female children, but it was clear that the old male bias had not yet been completely eradicated.

What may not be as obvious is how universal a phenomenon this is everywhere else. It is not only Chinese women who have to fight for basic survival and acceptance; their sisters elsewhere share the same plight to a greater or lesser degree.

Returning to one's homeland provokes different emotions for different people. Many become nostalgic for the mysterious past and just bask in the aura of the exotic Orient. Pleasant myth is far easier to accept than reality. But some find sobering thoughts in the midst of a changing society. The pace of social change in China is amazingly rapid these days, and it is not too far-fetched to predict its impact on the rest of the Far East, if not the world.

Writing these essays has occupied me for the last year. I knew I must start on a personal level. I cannot begin to do any analytic writing without recalling the individual stories told to me during my travels; without revealing too, my own family situations and baring my own soul. This has been a journey into my past, often revealing painful moments which are usually repressed and ignored. It has been, nevertheless, a necessary journey for me.

On the eve of another new year, I am finally sitting down to write to you. Across the miles, we share a joint destiny. It must be part of human destiny, for the very survival and growth of humankind depends on how the races and nations live and work together, and how men and women learn to share the same dreams. After years of pondering, my vision is clearing. It is not good enough to be equal to men and to take the same positions in society; we must do more by contributing more humane values and fresh strategies for creating a better world.

But we must start somewhere. Let me begin my stories.

Alice Murong Pu Lin, DSW
Albany, New York
December 1987

Part One

THE CHINESE FAMILY
BETWEEN TRADITION
AND MODERNITY

1

Childhood Whispers

The water surrounded me. I had fallen into the river. The tadpoles I had been trying to catch must have been darting away from me now. But I couldn't see a thing. I swallowed the river water, an unpleasant taste of underwater weeds. After that, I remembered nothing.

When I came to, I was being carried up the slope to my house on the outskirts of the city of Chengdu, on the back of a teenager, a girl in Girl Scout uniform. I felt my wet and clammy clothes and shoes clinging to my skin and feet. I had completely ruined the new red leather shoes Mother had bought for me for celebration of the traditional Children's Day. I was supposed to attend the school picnic later that day with my classmates from the kindergarten class. With a bottle and a notion of my own, I had slipped away to catch tadpoles in the river. Luckily for me the teenager had happened by just as I fell into the river, and rescued me. I was less than three at the time.

From my own partial and disjointed memories and Mother's reminiscences, I was probably not an easy child to raise. While I could turn on the charm and win over any adults in the family, I had a mind of my own and was very stubborn. It would show up in some unusual circumstances.

My entry into school was one example. Mother loved to tell how, at age two, I had followed my cousin Zhenli, three years my senior, into the kindergarten class and refused to leave. The teacher, a good friend of Mother's and unaccustomed to small children showing a keen interest in school, did not order me out. Instead, she offered me a special table and chair complete with her own drinking cup, and there I stayed.

I would go on to complete the first grade by age four, under the same unorthodox arrangement. Not that I was an exceptional student in those early years. My interest in school probably had more to do with group activities than anything else.

The city of Chengdu, where I was born, is in western Sichuan province. Here I spent the first few years of my life before we returned to Hubei province, my mother's birthplace. Life seemed easy and comfortable there, even with the Sino-Japanese War going on and lowered living standards. I was growing up in a completely female household, with Mother, First Aunt, my cousin Zhenli, and Grandmother Li. The occasional male visitors were usually close relatives. Nurtured and protected, I had no memory of pain or discomfort even when the adults were facing their own crises.

I remember one summer evening I was abruptly awakened by my first aunt and was rushed out, bed-covers and all. I looked up and saw a flaming red light through the window. A fire! In no time I was deposited safely on the grass of the front yard with the rest of the family. Together we watched a big fire in progress down the hill. It was the elementary school, the beloved school where I went daily for stories and cookies. I heard the adults' urgent conversation, but did not quite get the gist of their discussion. Still half asleep, I was fascinated by the bright glare, the smell of charred wood, the burning buildings. Years later I learned that arson had been suspected, evidently engineered by the superintendent of the school to cover up the irregular books he had kept, because he anticipated an outside audit. To me, however, that evening was more or less a summer interlude—I loved the colors of the sky above and felt safe in my first aunt's arms. Fear was foreign to me.

Children in China were often held and carried in the arms or on the backs of the adult women who could not afford to have their daily household chores interrupted. Carrying the child close to the body was convenient and comforting for both the adult and the child. Chinese men and women, however, rarely showed physical affection toward each other in public, contrary to their responses to children. I sensed, even then, that the adults played by an entirely different set of rules.

After the end of the Second World War in 1945, we all moved to grandmother's house in Wuhan, Hubei. There my second uncle and aunt gave me my first lessons in adulthood and its problems. They were the first couple I had the opportunity to observe close-up. Second Uncle was some sort of bank clerk. His marriage to Second Aunt, Mother's second eldest sister, was considered a good match: both families were Muslim. In addition, Second Uncle was from an educated, professional family, his sister being one of the few women at the time studying for a medical degree. Living next to Grandmother's house in

Wuhan, both Second Uncle and Aunt were regular visitors to the family. Second Aunt was a competent homemaker, her culinary skill was the equal of First Aunt's and her needlework surpassed that of most of her sisters. My mother was very fond of her second eldest sister. Both quick-witted and quick-tempered, they spent lots of time in each other's company. It seemed logical for me to stay overnight with Second Aunt's family when Mother's work took her out of town. It was to be an eye-opening experience for me.

Second Uncle evidently had his after-work routine down pat. Upon entering his front door he would call in a commanding voice for the chambermaid. "Spring Flower!" he would bellow, "Come and get me my slippers!" Spring Flower, a girl not more than fifteen or sixteen, would scurry forward with a pair of clean slippers and a warm hand towel. I was mesmerized by what I saw: Second Uncle's total dominance over everyone in the family and poor Spring Flower's thankless task. Not knowing the root of my feelings, I felt indignant for Spring Flower. Why did Second Uncle order her about as if he were so much more important? Why couldn't he get his own slippers? For reasons that were not clear to me at the time, since I was only about four or five, I never developed any warm feelings toward Second Uncle. I would hear whispered conversation between Mother and her sister, my second aunt, when they thought they were out of everyone's hearing (not counting a little girl like me). They insinuated some irregular activities on the part of Second Uncle, that he was not shy about making advances toward female servants of his household nor visiting certain brothels in town. Typically, Second Aunt would lament her fate, being trapped in this predicament, and Mother would be consoling. I was puzzled by the complexity of the adult world and the seemingly help-less positions in which women found themselves.

Nor was I to escape, even as a tiny girl, from being an easy target for male attention. One of my older cousins, a teenage boy, was developing an unnatural interest in me. When we were out of the adults' sight, he would call me in private his "future darling little wife." He would bring me candies and cupcakes and show me nude pictures of movie stars. When we were alone he would expose himself and make lewd gestures. Sensing these to be inappropriate behaviors, though I was genuinely fond of his storytelling, I finally told Mother about these episodes.

Mother was putting me to bed one evening when I told her what my cousin had said and done that day. Face white, she got up from the bed and walked out, muttering that she was going to have a good talk with his mother. Moments later she came back and we had a talk, mother to daughter. Mother told me that men always tried to take advantage of women and that this had been true through-out the history of China, and that she was glad I had con-fided in her. She commented on the absence of a male in the house and wondered about Father's return to China.

Father did return, in 1947, two years after the war ended. Mother and I took a riverboat from Wuhan to Nanjing, where Father had set up housekeeping for us. On the boat, two young men, complete strangers, struck up a conversa-tion with me. Impressed with my ability to read and write at such a young age (I was probably showing off as usual), they asked me to write down the names of my parents, at which point Mother quickly walked over to retrieve me from them. She seemed nervous and worried, and insisted that I sit with her during the remainder of the journey. I sensed her discomfort and obeyed, not totally understanding the natural fear of single women traveling in China during the post-war era. The social order was not strong enough to assure young women of their personal safety and stories about extortion, kidnapping, and worse were fairly common.

Mother probably had another good reason to be anxious. She was on her way to meet her husband after more than four years of separation. She kept reminding me to call my father by his name when I met him. I nodded. Father had been only a concept to me up to then. He was the greeting cards during holidays and birthdays, pictures on the wall, and presents in the boxes sent from overseas. I knew I had a father in the United States. I was told he was there to pursue graduate studies. I repeated it each time people asked me, but I had no feeling about him as a person.

I finally had a glimpse of Father. A tall, dark man. He came onto the riverboat after an inordinate wait and waved to Mother, who had become very emotional upon spotting him. I stood next to Mother on the deck and looked at this stranger. He was not like any of the pictures I had seen, for he seemed much bigger and stronger. I saw them hugging each other. Then Mother patted my shoulder, turning me to face him and said, "This is your father, Rongrong." I found my voice and called him "Dad," as if in a dream state. He picked me up to give me a big hug. Then all three of us left the boat. In his shiny new jeep, Father took us, our baggage, and all our years without him, to our new residence. Our jeep crossed the wide boulevards of Nanjing, with huge trees along the roadsides. It started to drizzle, clouding the street lamps with a heavy mist. I had no idea where we were going, but I knew instinctively that this stranger, my father, was taking us to a dry and comfortable place, a place that would hold much hope and promise.

Father had joined the Nationalist Air Force after graduating from the Shanghai Communication and Transportation University with a degree in aeronautical engineering. He had easily won the award to study in the United States, sponsored by the air force as part of the government's move to modernize. He had subsequently earned a master's degree in aeronautical engineering from Brooklyn Polytechnic Institute and went on for a doctorate. But his stay was cut short by his commitment to the air force to return to his duties.

Father returned to his homeland with new ideas and strong ethical standards. Promoted to the rank of lieutenant major in the air force, he found himself pursued by staff seeking personal favors and businessmen seeking lucrative contracts. Father's response to these attempts was a uniform rejection coupled with his eloquent speech on the patriotic duty of citizens to abide by the rules of proper conduct. I remember one afternoon when a lower-ranking officer brought two boxes of imported goods, a rare find during the last years of the Nationalist regime when inflation and food scarcities hit all urban centers without warning. The man was hoping to get Father to grant him a personal favor at work. Father shoved him and the two boxes of gifts out the front door. He sternly told him never to return, because he was a disgrace to the entire air force. Mother and I rushed out to see the commotion. I saw the hurt and awkward expression on this poor man's face and Father's explosive anger. My father had a real temper, I noted to myself.

But most of the time Father was a caring and compassionate man. Friends and colleagues came to the house seeking his counsel on domestic as well as work-related problems. Those in managerial positions were responsible not only for the staff at work but also for their family affairs at home. This was true in the military services, business, and the academic community.

Having been without a father for more than four years —Father had left when I was a few months old—I was delighted to have him with us. I quickly adjusted to the new routine of rushing to the door when he came home from work, and going out with him on summer nights to sit under the sky. Father would carry out a big bamboo seat and I would sit on it while he told Mother and me stories—stories about far away places and things he had done over the years. He would show us a miniature statue of the Empire State Building in New York City. He told me there were miniature people hiding in it—for years I believed his stories and would look gingerly through the little windows to get a glimpse of these tiny people. When I was too tired to stay awake I would fall asleep on the bamboo seat and be carried back to the house. We also had outings to the Memorial tomb of Sun Yat-sen, the tomb for the founding emperor of the Ming Dynasty, and to the Xuanwu Lake for a boat ride.

We shared the big house in Nanjing with another family, that of Father's schoolmate in the United States, who had also returned to China to start his own manufacturing factory. The common ground between the two families was the central courtyard. So once again I was to be witness to the goings-on of a typical courtyard, where visitors came in to chat, where families met face to face, privacy temporarily forgotten, where the fundamentals of human life and relationships could be so easily observed.

Our neighbors, the Zhang family, had two children, a boy and a girl, about my age. We became fast friends in no time. I took a special liking to the boy, a couple of years my senior, who had a pair of lovely dimples and big, brown eyes. I spent more time however with his sister, both of us sharing an enthusiasm for baby dolls.

The Zhang family had a maternal grandmother living with them, and soon my paternal grandmother came to live with us, bringing her newly adopted son, Jing, a ten-year-old boy. Grandmother Pu, having raised four sons and one daughter, had decided to adopt another boy to keep her company at home.

The two grandmothers were treated in totally contrasting ways. Grandmother Zhang had no standing in the family; she was maid, cook, and washerwoman for her daughter's family. Frugal and tightfisted, the Zhangs insisted that Grandmother Zhang use the rainwater to wash clothes, whereas most families with means would get fresh water from the faucet down the road, paying a price for it. I remember watching Grandmother Zhang doing a full load of laundry in the central courtyard, her hands swollen and scaly, her silent tears dropping into the wooden bucket. "Your grandmother has such a good son and daughter-in-law. She does not have any housework. But look at me," she said, holding out her hands. "Look at my poor hands!" I would feel so sorry for her that I would rush to my room to get her some of my butter cookies, the only token I could think of to console her. "I wish you were my granddaughter," she would say smiling, after eating my cookies, for she was not allowed nibbles between meals in her own family. I felt so good about relieving some of her pain that I thought about soliciting help for her from the family, but obviously I was not getting very far in changing her plight.

The visit of Grandmother Pu was itself not without trauma. At an advanced age, after a life of hard labor, Grandmother Pu was looking forward to joining her third son in family harmony. She would find that life with Father, Mother, me, and her newly adopted son was not an easy one to get used to. The boy, Jing, in frail health, was chronically incontinent. Given his lack of interest in school, and the need to change his bed linen often, Mother began to complain to Father about the burden of caring for him. Grandmother Pu, on the other hand, was protective of her adopted son and saw Mother's duties as the expected services of a daughter-in-law. She was particularly troubled by Mother's quick temper and outspokenness. Mother and Grandmother Pu spoke different dialects and had difficulty communicating with each other, which compounded the tension between them. Caught in the middle, Father would be the peacemaker when he could, and ignore them both when he could not.

One night I was awakened by voices in my parents' room. Half-awake, I got the drift of their argument: Mother was complaining about Grandmother Pu and her adopted son, Jing, while Father was getting defensive. Then I heard Mother's muffled crying. The next morning when Mother came to dress me for school, I asked her what had been the matter, but by then she had evidently resolved whatever differences she might have had with Father and was her cheerful self again.

I knew that, despite this argument, my parents cared for each other. After a while, feeling homesick and uncomfortable in the cold winter of Nanjing, Grandmother Pu took her adopted son Jing home, back to Guangzhou, where the climate was warmer and more pleasant for her. Life for us in Nanjing seemed to return to normal. My parents would go out together in the evening to a show or to dance. I was often left by myself in the house with instructions not to touch the electric stove. And I would venture out into the courtyard to chat with the Zhang children. All three of us would sit on our individual wooden benches under the sky and make up stories about our future.

It was the same sky, on those evenings when I was alone, that I had watched while living with Grandmother Li in her big house in Wuhan and it was the same flaming red sky over Chengdu, when I and my family watched the fire at the elementary school from the top of the hill; it was the same sky under which I listened to Father's storytelling. For me, the sky was the universe, where dreams could be pinned to the stars, where fantasies could run wild and deep—the sky of my childhood.

2

Grandmother Had No Name

My maternal grandmother had no name of her own. I never knew the significance of this until I returned again to China in 1982, my second visit since Liberation.

The fact is, I had learned years ago that grandmother had no name. During my early teens I came upon photos of her among old family documents. Two photos stood out in my memory. One was a three-by-five glossy black-and-white picture, showing her in a velvet turban with a piece of jewelry, probably jade, right in the center. Grandmother had a rather long face, unlike most moon-faced Chinese women of her generation, and her features looked distinctly Western—large double-lidded eyes, high-bridged nose, high cheek bones, and a wide mouth. I thought she looked at once exotic and beautiful. Only years later did I associate her Western features with her Muslim background. Another photo had her sitting in a rattan chair in the courtyard, with her children standing beside her, all five girls and one boy. She looked powerful but lonely in this picture, without Grandfather's presence—he had passed away when the children were young. As I searched through the old family albums and documents, I saw an old household registration, commonly used in those days as a substitute for individual identification, in which Grandmother was listed as Mrs. Li—no first name, no maiden name, just Mrs. Li.

I remember asking Mother if Grandmother's first name had been inadvertently left out. Mother explained that it was the proper way of registering married women in the old days—a woman was known only as a wife in her new family. Mother did not recall Grandmother's given name, if she had one, for she was always Mu-ma to Mother, Mu-ma meaning Mom in the local Wuhan dialect. Though I thought at the time the situation odd and archaic, I did not pursue my curiosity further. I was then more interested in Grandmother's life as wife in the Li family.

Mother told me that Grandfather Li had come from an old Chinese Muslim family whose ancestors had emigrated to China via the old Silk Road, ending up in Xian centuries ago. The family later moved eastward into Hubei, in central China. Li was not their original Muslim name, but the imperial name of a Ming emperor, given to Grandfather's ancestors in recognition for good services performed for the emperor.

This association with the imperial family would have a profound impact on the occupational choices of the Li men. No longer limited to the merchant trade, they began to assume various government and military positions during the next centuries. By the time Grandfather was born, his immediate ancestors had developed a strong family tradition in military service. Thus it was not surprising that Grandfather found himself enrolled in the Wuhan Military

Academy, demonstrating a keen interest in a military career. Grandfather was one of the few graduates of the Academy chosen to go on to study in Japan. But to his deep regret, he never made the trip. Instead, he settled down in Wuhan with the Muslim girl chosen for him by his parents, a girl he had not met before the wedding.

Arranged marriage was still practiced well into this century. This could be done through a matchmaker or arranged by the parents of both families, depending on their relative social status, economic ability, and the ties between the two families. As a child, I was only dimly aware of the trauma a couple must have gone through facing the unknown, namely each other and their new life together. One sunny morning, while living with Grandmother, I joined other children to watch a wedding procession in the neighborhood. The bride, under a heavy veil of scarlet brocade covering her entire head and face, was being led to a waiting carriage by her family, her mother sobbing incessantly. Face unseen, the bride also seemed visibly shaken. Puzzled by the sad and tearful scene, I followed the carriage to the house of the bridegroom's family. Watching brides arrive at their new residence was a favorite pastime for neighborhood children. They had practically surrounded the house, fighting to get a closer look at this bride. I joined the crowd and after considerable struggle reached the bedroom window. I looked in. The new bride was sitting on the bed, wiping tears from under her veil. I was disappointed in not getting a good look at her, but I heard an older child next to me muttering, "Wait until she sees the bridegroom. He's as ugly as a toad."

After his marriage to Grandmother in 1904, Grandfather's military career began to prosper. He was soon appointed the military envoy to supervise affairs along the border with Burma, far away from his family in central China. Rarely home, he left the running of the household to Grandmother (although, despite his protracted absences, they still produced six children). As we expected in those days, Grandfather soon felt the need to set up a household away from home; he was seriously contemplating taking a concubine. When the news of his intention reached Grandmother, she wasted no time. Despite this common practice among well-off males, Grandmother was not about to be left out of the arrangement. Feet bound and inexperienced in travel, she gathered her expanding family brood and headed for the Burmese border, traveling one thousand miles to get there. The concubine-to-be was so terrified of Grandmother's arrival and her potential negative vote that she pulled out all the stops to make Grandmother's stay comfortable. Mother recounted the first encounter: the middle-aged matron and the slip of a girl sizing up each other. The concubine, recognizing her own inferior status in the family hierarchy, knelt down in a deep kowtow to pledge her loyalty to her "elder sister" and to their master. Grandmother soon warmed to the girl's attempts at sisterly affection and felt comfortable enough to return home to Hubei, only to learn a few months later that the concubine had eloped with Grandfather's lieutenant. One woman had out-witted another, and in the end, outsmarted the man in their lives.

Grandfather and Grandmother seemed to become closer after the affair of the concubine. Grandmother declared that she needed to take over the matter of looking for another concubine. For whatever reason, she never found one. Grandfather, on the other hand, was growing tired of his constant travels, and contemplated an early retirement from the service.

Mother was close to Grandfather Li. Being the fourth daughter, she was treated more like a boy by Grandfather, who by then had given up any hope for a son—he would go on to have another daughter before the only son was born—and seemed to take particular liking to Mother's outgoing personality. "My fourth one," he would call out to her on returning from an extended absence. "See what I've got here for you!" Mother would jump into his lap, an unusually affectionate gesture toward a father for a little girl at that time, and delightedly examine the souvenir he had brought for her. Grandfather's constant travels had also expanded his knowledge and awareness of the outside world. A believer in education, even for girls, he encouraged Mother's schooling. Hence, unlike the three sisters before her, Mother was able to receive a regular public education. Grandfather Li also brought ideas about the "natural feet" movement from the Guangzhou region, where women at the turn of the century had stopped the practice of foot-binding. None of his daughters would have to go through this inhuman treatment, he declared, even if their prospect of marriage was diminished by a pair of big feet. While Grandfather was loud and demanding, accustomed to commanding armies during his military career, he was unusually gentle around Grandmother and deferred to her in most domestic decisions. Grandmother, on the other hand, secure in her position in the family, never flaunted her hold on Grandfather in front of the children.

Grandmother held the purse strings in the family, a practice common among the Chinese women of her generation, based on the belief that men should take care of the affairs outside the home, women in the home. After Grandfather retired from military service, he decided to go into the confectionery business, but not being a businessman nor interested in becoming one, he quickly lost the family fortune. Mother recalled the final years of Grandfather's management of the business: food was freely given away to friends and relatives; baskets of black sesame seeds, used in cookies and pastries, were pilfered from the store with no accounting; the books were in disarray. This would have a profound impact on Grandfather. The once powerful military commander became an unhappy old man, squandering his time in the teahouse swapping stories with old friends. Grandmother, on the other hand, remained stoic and serene throughout those financially turbulent years. So adept in financial matters, she single-handedly raised the six children without outside financial help.

I grew up in Grandmother's household. Mother went home to stay after my birth, while Father was studying in the United States. By then, most of Grandmother's children had left home. The only son had died during the Sino-Japanese War as a pilot in the air force, and his surviving daughter, Zhenli, three years older than I, had been left with Grandmother by her mother, who had eloped with another man after my uncle's death. Also living with Grandmother, in addition to Mother, Zhenli, and myself, was First Aunt who had returned home following the death of her husband, long before the rest of us joined Grandmother in her big house. To supplement the family income, Grandmother had to rent sections of the house to distant relatives. I remember watching the comings and goings of countless uncles, aunts, and cousins from the center courtyard. In my childhood memories, Grandmother was a petite, frail woman, moving quietly in the background, who in her final years had relinquished the major household responsibilities to First Aunt, her eldest daughter. Grandmother seemed to speak little, and when she did, it was in a low whisper.

With her reduced responsibilities at home, Grandmother spent a lot of time with me and my cousin Zhenli. Her bound feet limited her movements. She had to walk slowly and every step put a sharp pain through her entire body, so Zhenli and I would act as her substitute for a walking cane whenever we ventured outside together. She had developed a love for the waterpipe, a popular activity among ladies of the leisure class, and I was assigned the task of making long straws from yellow rice paper to light her pipe. After supper, we would all sit in the back-yard, watching the stars in the sky, listening to her storytelling, and the burbling of her waterpipe. I would often be lulled to sleep and carried back into the house. But, more often than not, after a long story, Grandmother would ask me to massage her back. "I want those tiny fists pounding on my back, Rongrong," she would say to me, and I would oblige her by using all my might to pound her backbones as hard as I could. Most of the time I thought of Grandmother as a hopeless and dependent old woman. I would be proved wrong soon enough.

The occasion was the visit from my paternal grandmother, Grandmother Pu. A native of Guangzhou province, she had big feet, spoke the hard-to-understand Cantonese, and, worst of all, was a pork-eater—a non-Muslim woman. Evidently Mother had broken with Muslim tradition by marrying a non-Muslim from another province, an event close to being open warfare with the parents in a Muslim family. Since Mother usually got what she wanted, she had gone ahead and married my father despite her family's opposition, and Grandmother Li had to become resigned to having a non-Muslim son-in-law. With this as a backdrop, the visit from Grandmother Pu was a critical one for Grandmother Li, who was determined to show utmost civility and hospitality. Having met Grandmother Pu before and having picked up some of the Cantonese dialect, I was the chosen family interpreter for the two grandmothers. The most immediate concern was food preparation, since Grandmother Pu loved her pork dishes and Grandmother Li forbade any pork products in the house. However, Grandmother Li hoped to convince Grandmother Pu that the healthy, delicate Muslim foods—Qingzheng cuisine— would be sufficient for her during her short stay with us. Grandmother Pu, on the other hand, had very little awareness of the importance of this issue and was soon asking for cooking utensils for herself so that she could cook in a separate section of the house. Eager to help and not recognizing the severity of the situation, I obtained the necessary cooking utensils for her. When the aroma of pork—the "evil smell"—penetrated the thin walls of Grandmother Pu's room and escaped into the central courtyard, Grandmother Li became outraged. Along with my hapless Mother, I was summoned to Grandmother Li's room. Sitting on top of her high rosewood bed, Grandmother sternly told me I had offended Allah's wishes and that I was a naughty, sinful girl. I stammered, "But . . . Grandmother Pu can't have our kind of food," but was stopped short by the cold stare, the only time I had faced real anger from Grandmother Li. Mother intervened at the appropriate moment and quickly ushered me out of Grandmother's room.

It was in 1982, when I visited Grandmother's house for the first time as an adult, that I began to see her in a new light. Here I was, standing in what had once been the central courtyard, the decayed stone pavement worn and darkened by years of neglect and abuse, recalling it as it had been more than three decades ago, with its very different inhabitants. The blurred image of Grandmother, in photos and childhood memories, became clearer. This exotic and mysterious woman had once put her life and soul into this house, but she did it in silence and anonymity. She came to the house nameless, and she left without leaving her name. Yet I did not imagine Grandmother sad and wistful, nor angry and resentful. She went about her own business quietly accepting it all. The imprint of her influence could still be felt decades after her departure.

As I reflected on this during my brief visit to Grandmother's house, I passed through her old bedroom, now occupied by a distant aunt. I looked in. The same rosewood bed was still there, with a starched white mosquito net hanging from the ceiling. Suddenly an old image came back to me. I saw Grandmother sitting on the bed, her bound feet on a stool, unwrapping her bandage—a daily ritual that never ceased to fascinate me. I saw her concentrated attention to her poor deformed toes, bent deeply into the soles of her feet, as she slowly and meticulously put her unwrapped feet in a basin of warm water. Fresh flower petals floated on top of the basin, adding to the aroma of the fragrant oil Grandmother had put in the basin to soften her feet. She looked up and smiled at me. She seemed so proud and so undaunted.

3

First Aunt—The Tragic Heroine

Whenever I think of my first aunt, I am reminded of the passages in typical Chinese romantic novels depicting the first day in the life of a newlywed girl in the old society.

Awakened before dawn, she slipped out of her bed quietly so as not to disturb her husband's slumber. The dim early morning light shot through the rice-papered windows onto the mirror on the dressing table. She made herself up meticulously before preparing the morning tea for her new parents. She could not help but notice the critical scrutiny from her mother-in-law as the tea was served, who was undoubtedly looking for clues that the newlyweds had been properly active the night before.

Like the heroine, my first aunt went through the tormenting experience of a young girl married into a powerful family of the 1920s. But, unlike the brides of the fictional romances, her marriage did not have a happy ending. She was a victim of marriage throughout her life.

First Aunt was sixteen when she was married into a Muslim family more prominent than her own. Her father, my grandfather Li, had considered the match suitable because First Aunt was to wed the eldest son of an important family, an enviable position for any girl seeking a marriage prospect. According to Chinese tradition, the eldest son, in addition to occupying the senior position among the siblings, holds the second most powerful rank in the family hierarchy. Second only to the family patriarch, he stands to inherit the bulk of the family fortune. By then, Grandfather's confectionery business had been failing steadily. For him, marrying off a daughter, particularly the eldest, was a logical step to alleviate the burdens of a financially troubled family.

According to First Aunt's own account, she knew nothing about her future husband except for his being the oldest son. As was typically the case with arranged marriages, she was in no position to voice her own reaction to the match. At age sixteen she was considered old enough to marry, and marry she did.

The first shock for First Aunt following the marriage was learning about her husband's physical condition. At a young age he had contracted tuberculosis and was now an invalid with a heavy opium addiction. Apparently his family had considered the marriage the proper way to turn around his poor state of health. The use of a wedding to bring good luck to the family and the bridegroom was called *chongxi* or "filling up happiness." His family had kept the illness from outsiders, including First Aunt's family. Needless to say, Grandfather was furious that he had been tricked into accepting the marriage proposal, but the shame of terminating a marriage after its consummation was so strong that he could not take any action. Grand-mother Li, though pained by her daughter's unfortunate position, attributed the circumstances to fate. She advised First Aunt to be patient and loyal to her new family.

As if this discovery of her husband's condition was not enough, First Aunt found herself a nursemaid to her invalid husband who, on days when he was more lucid and drug-free, would demand her total attention in waiting on him. He rarely left his bedroom, because his condition had ex-cused him from taking up a vocation and the family con-tinued to support his idle lifestyle. First Aunt would stay with him, filling his opium pipe, bringing food to his bed and escorting him to the toilet when he was too weak to help himself. He was especially tyrannical in his demand that First Aunt, not any maid or manservant, be the one to perform the most intimate tasks for him.

As a young bride, First Aunt also had the obligatory morning ritual of kowtowing to her parents-in-law and serving them breakfast tea. The breakfast tea ritual, prac-ticed well into the middle of this century, served to demon-strate the power hierarchy in the bride's new family. Not only were the bride's delicate manners in serving tea ap-praised, but so was the bride herself, like a specimen to be tested and molded—not one strand of hair out of place, nor any misapplication of makeup, nor improper choice of clothing. Otherwise, the bride would be confronted with her shortcomings and told to correct the deficiencies.

It was difficult for me to picture First Aunt as the delicate, ill-fated bride, for when I knew her, she had lost all her youthful looks. She was a rather masculine woman, big-boned and tall (considered uncomely in those days), with an awkward gait and unusually high cheek-bones and square jaw, her straight hair tied up in a severe bun at the nape. She seldom smiled at us and often gave her horrifying stare at our mischievousness. I and my cousin Zhenli were more than once intimidated into silent obedience by First Aunt's stare. Only years later did I understand the self-protective function of her lack of femininity. Her gender had brought her nothing but misery in life.

My aunt's first year with her in-laws was oppressive, especially for a girl of sixteen. At the same time, contact with her own family was limited and frowned upon. A bride's return to her old family, other than at the acceptable holiday season, was considered a betrayal of her new family. Not being able to share her miserable state of mind, least of all with her husband, First Aunt took the step many women before her had taken. She attempted suicide by swallowing a large amount of opium from her husband's supply. It was the fear of scandal that finally brought a change of attitude in her new family. First Aunt was laid up for a while, to recuperate from the failed suicide, and had some respite for the first time since entering the household. Miraculously, she also became pregnant, thereby enjoying the pampered state of an expectant mother who drew attention and delicate treatment from all, to ensure the birth of a healthy child.

Her good fortune in being left alone did not last long, however. Before long her husband died of an opium overdose, while First Aunt was still pregnant. The only son, Lianfeng, would be born without knowing his father. What went through First Aunt's mind at her husband's death would never be known, for she never discussed it with Grandmother Li or her four sisters. Grandfather Li passed away soon after, in the same year, leaving First Aunt completely at the mercy of her in-laws.

Luckily, giving birth to a healthy son was viewed as the single most important accomplishment a married woman could make, and this dramatically changed First Aunt's status with her in-laws. Having suffered the loss of the eldest son, they now devoted their full attention and care to the eldest grandson. Thus First Aunt, despite the absence of any male support from her own family, was able to gather some strength on her own, and her life became less stressful for a few years.

But then her in-laws passed away. A fight for the family fortune erupted. With a large number of relatives fighting for their share of the family fortune, First Aunt, being meek and agreeable, did not fare well in the ugly struggle for control of the estate. In the end, she was given a big family house as the sole inheritance for her son and herself. Discouraged and anxious to sever ties with her husband's family, she sold the house and moved in with Grandmother Li. The two widows, mother and daughter, formed a team of mutual support to raise the rest of the family, four girls and one boy, plus First Aunt's own son.

Mother, the fourth of five daughters, was brought up more by her eldest sister, First Aunt, than by her own mother, partly because the ten years difference between them fostered First Aunt's maternal affection toward her younger sister, and partly because Mother relied heavily on First Aunt's support during her student years. First Aunt, though largely self-taught, was more educated than her own mother, and could take a more enlightened view of Mother's carefree ways in school and her less-than-brilliant performance as a student. First Aunt also helped Mother with her home economics assignments from school, for Mother was hopelessly inadequate when it came to cooking and sewing and all the other domestic activities expected of young girls of her day. During Grandmother Li's final years, the household responsibilities had been transferred to First Aunt, who took them over effortlessly; she became the true matriarch of the Li family. Though skilled in sewing and needlework, she did these mostly for others, she herself maintaining the same plain-looking exterior.

First Aunt also cared for me during my stay in Grandmother's house, while Mother was working and Father was studying abroad. As the years went on, Mother became more critical of First Aunt's ways as she outgrew her dependence on her. She was particularly dissatisfied with the way First Aunt dressed me. "You make her look like a peasant boy!" Mother often complained. Due to her work schedule and the distance of her work place, she was only home on weekends. Thanks to my Muslim lineage, I was born with a full head of curly hair and Mother took great delight in fixing my hair with ribbons and bows. She was therefore shocked, on returning home one weekend to find me totally bald. First Aunt had decided I should have my head shaved, like all little girls, to get rid of the "baby hair" and foster the healthy growth of thicker, straight black hair. Mother was beside herself. She cried and carried on for days. Fortunately, my hair grew back with some wave, even into adulthood, a saving grace for my first aunt.

First Aunt was without a doubt the most popular and helpful neighbor in the district where we lived. Always quick to assist anyone in need, she cooked for the poor, helped nurse the sickly, and seemed to be forever doing things for others. While indulgent of her younger sisters, she was rather severe with their children, my cousin Zhenli and me. We were the ones always underfoot whenever she was busy cooking or sewing. First Aunt's cold stare was employed as a special tactic to deal with our mischievousness. With eyes bulging almost out of their sockets, she would let out a stern yell, "Zhenli! Rongrong! That's enough!" Without fail, Zhenli and I were brought into line.

I had the uneasy impression that First Aunt favored Zhenli over me, probably from First Aunt's protective instinct of giving more care to the less fortunate. Zhenli was born without a father, and her mother abandoned her to elope with someone else when Zhenli was just a few months old, whereas I had Mother's undivided attention, and a distant father abroad who showered me with presents. Besides, Zhenli, though a few years older, cried easily and was often scolded for her frequent crying bouts, contrary to my unflappable, stubborn demeanor. I seldom cried, even under trying circumstances. I also managed to get on the good side of the adults in the family and stayed out of trouble more skillfully than Zhenli.

Zhenli and I fought a great deal. As naive and cruel children sometimes do, I would let Zhenli know during some of our ferocious arguments that she didn't have the love of real parents, which inevitably reduced her to tears. First Aunt would come to the rescue by slapping me on the behind or taking Zhenli away from me.

In 1979, when I visited Zhenli again, she had left Wuhan, to work in Beijing, after graduation from college. Neither of us had seen each other for thirty years, and I was finally able to apologize for my childhood follies. Zhenli, her own memories altered by the subsequent suffering of the Cultural Revolution, seemed perplexed by my apology: "What are you talking about, Rongrong? Those years were the best times in my life!"

After Liberation in 1949, First Aunt had continued to live with Grandmother Li and Zhenli in the same old house in Wuhan, while my family had gone to Taiwan with the Nationalist government. Cut off by the communications blockade between the mainland and Taiwan, Mother could no longer write home and we lost contact. Zhenli told me, when we met again at last, that First Aunt never had any true joy in her life. Her only son, Lianfeng, had been captured by an aboriginal tribe during the retreat of his Nationalist army unit, and First Aunt died without ever seeing him again.

In the same big house in Wuhan, Zhenli and First Aunt became the sole inhabitants after the death of Grandmother Li. Fortunately the death was uneventful and a Muslim burial was arranged with the approval of the new government. Without any means of support, First Aunt had continued to rent sections of the house to relatives and friends until even this meager income was discontinued when the government took over all private properties and allocated them to other residents of the neighborhood. First Aunt took in sewing and laundry to help support herself and Zhenli, who, as the daughter of a war hero, received a small stipend and free education.

Zhenli recalled the harsh years during the Great Leap Forward movement in the 1950s when the entire country had a serious food shortage. Zhenli had longed for a red sweater for the upcoming Chinese New Year but dared not hope to get one in light of the financial situation at home. Sensing her desire, First Aunt had said, "I'll see what I can do. Don't you worry about a thing." A few months later, returning home from school, Zhenli found a flaming-red sweater, brand-new and inviting, on top of her bed, evidently the fruit of First Aunt's ingenious ways of saving money and knitting the sweater herself. Zhenli showed me the same red sweater on my 1979 visit to her apartment in Beijing. The flaming red had faded, both elbows were patched and worn, but it was kept clean and fresh, carefully wrapped in a plastic bag, as a reminder of a lovely, selfless lady.

Zhenli told me of First Aunt's sudden death, from a fall and fatal stroke. First Aunt had just returned from the store, carrying a heavy bag of rice, when she slipped on the doorstep and fell, never regaining consciousness. Zhenli was in school when this happened. Barely a teenager and not very strong physically, Zhenli managed to have First Aunt taken to a local hospital, where First Aunt was pronounced dead. A Muslim burial was arranged by Zhenli with help from the neighbors. All in their individual ways had received help from First Aunt who, in her last few years of life, had in fact been elected leader of the powerful neighborhood association, and had been considered one of the best local leaders.

The day of the funeral, everyone in the entire neighborhood turned up to pay their respects to First Aunt, each with individual memories of this woman, their friend and helper. The entire alley was lined with people who had come to pay their last tribute, their public recognition of her selfless devotion to family and community. It is sad that she could not witness this public testimony, and that mother and I could not be present to express to her our joint gratitude for all those years of loving care. Sad too, that she died before her only son returned home after long years of hard labor for the aboriginal tribe and then in a reform camp, that she never saw the pain and tears he brought to her tombstone after being away for more than thirty years.

She could never know how I had observed her and learned from her, that her example would finally teach me the courage and determination to break free from the shackles of tradition, the bondage, the suffering that women of her generation had endured in powerless silent dignity.

4

Love and Marriage in China

U ntil a few short decades ago, the notion that love between a man and a woman would lead to marriage was as alien a concept to the Chinese as the assumption that women had any control over whom they would marry. Marrying, according to the traditional Chinese view, was a family business, not the couple's affair. Having a daughter was considered a "money-losing proposition," given the lack of return on the investment. After raising a daughter, to marry her off required a dowry and losing her permanently to another family, for once married, the daughter's identity was with her husband's family. A woman was taught from birth that she must prepare herself for lifelong servitude, to serve her parents and elders while at home, her husband and in-laws once married, and her own sons after the death of her husband. The only redeeming hope for a woman was to become a mother-in-law herself so the cycle could go on.

Such was the typical course of life for a young woman ready for matrimony in the old China. It is no small wonder that I do not remember any stories of happy brides. Brides in my memory were inevitably linked to separation, tears, fear, and uncertainty about the future. My mother, who was close to her elder sister, my first aunt, and with whom she had shared a bedroom, followed my first aunt's wedding carriage out of the door, crying and calling her name, so distraught that she fell down and got a bad cut that left a scar on her left eyebrow that she carries to this day.

Whether one married "up" or "down", the expectations for the new bride varied little. Until she became a mother, preferably of a son, she occupied the lowest rank in the family hierarchy, even lower than that of the unmarried sister of her husband. Any harmony between herself and her new husband was purely by chance. Usually the two barely knew each other before the wedding.

The matchmakers might occasionally provide an opportunity for "viewing" each other before the couple was married, usually under the scrutiny of both families, and from a distance. Tales about how the bride might camouflage her physical shortcomings from a cursory and distant viewing made up interesting after-dinner conversations while I was growing up. The viewing of the potential mate was a custom practiced even in modern China in some regions. If the impressions of the viewing were favorable, with again the families having more to say than the couple, and if the other conditions were met, the couple would be considered "spoken."

Under such circumstances, romantic attachments before marriage were rare. If emotional bonding between husband and wife were ever established, it occurred only after the marriage. This phenomenon largely explained the relatively few literary works devoted to the celebration of romantic love. Most literary works have described friendship among men, men in relationship with nature, and filial loyalty. There have been some exceptions to the rule. The famous and talented poet Li Qingzhao from the Song Dynasty wrote about missing her husband far away:

> The west wind curls back the curtain,
> I am more fragile than the golden chrysanthemum.

Another Song poet wrote about how much he enjoyed helping his wife make up her eyebrows in the morning, but such references to the marital relationship are extremely rare in classical Chinese poetry.

A young woman was brought up to accept her destiny in a subservient role in marriage. As a general rule from age seven on, a girl was segregated from members of the opposite sex, except for her immediate male relatives. Indeed all contact with the outside world was limited to the immediate household. In this closed and controlled setting, a young woman learned obedience and tolerance for an uncertain future. The alternative of remaining single was not available. Custom decreed that a woman must marry. The stigma attached to spinsterhood was severe enough to strongly discourage staying single.

The young woman was taught to value two essential virtues for a married woman: patience and self-denial. To navigate the myriad relationships in an extended family required patience. To fulfill the daily demands of others required self-sacrifice. Both patience and self-sacrifice were considered necessary to maintain harmony in the new household, and harmony was the ideal state of married life. These values were not defined by the individual, but by the family as a unit, and a woman's needs took a back seat to those of others.

A young man was brought up with different lessons. He was taught to be worthy of carrying the male ancestor's name by achieving a certain position in society, supporting his family, and being loyal to his parents. Even supporting the family, a universal expectation for men in a male-dominant society, did not need to be a burden solely for the Chinese man. If he were unemployed or fell on hard times he could turn to his wife for support, particularly if the available jobs were distasteful to him. It was not unusual for the wife to go out to do menial labor to support the family while the husband waited at home for more suitable employment. Public sympathy, however, was not with the woman, who was presumed merely to be fulfilling her wifely duties in serving her husband and her family.

In the traditional Chinese family a male, the head of the household, always had, at least titular, supreme power over the others. In actual practice however power was often more widely distributed. Chinese women learned long ago how to gain influence in the family. In financial affairs, for example, women had the primary responsibility and made the decisions in running the household. The more well-off families hired a family treasurer, an employee who over time might gain the status of an accepted family member but who deferred in major decisions to the lady of the house. In most families the wife took care of budgeting and bookkeeping, following the doctrine that men should mind business outside and women inside the home. My grandmother Li held the purse strings in the family. My mother and all her sisters managed their own families' budgets. My mother's friends all enjoyed this responsibility. The husbands would regularly turn over their earnings to their wives, keeping a small allowance for themselves. Even the exceptional case of a husband managing the family finances was attributed to the individual ineptitude of the wife in financial affairs, rather than the preferred choice for a man. For larger, more complicated households, the wife and concubines—particularly the concubines—would hoard some "secret house money" for rainy days, unbeknownst to their husband and master.

Traditional Chinese women participated actively, in educating the young, especially during the children's formative years. Depending on the economic status of the family, a wet nurse might become the mothering figure for the young child. A child might have more contact with the wet nurse than with his own biological mother.

The traditional function of a Chinese marriage, as for many it still is today, was to extend the family bloodline. Men and women married in order to procreate. A secondary function was social and economic. Marriage was the basic social support for the individual, since most social activities took place within the family and the family unit provided the basic economic means of caring for the young. Marriage, then, in traditional as well as in modern China, was never perceived as a romantic union between a man and a woman, but as a social and economic family affair. Modern men and women do indeed fall in love before the wedding, but love is not considered the primary requisite for a successful marriage.

In fact, even for Chinese men, romantic love did not occupy an important place. The main function of sex was to carry on the family line. A second wife might be taken simply because the first wife had not borne any sons.

The relationships among the husband and his several wives were always intriguing. Chinese women in the same household evidently learned to be tolerant of one another. I remember my close relationship as a teenager with an elderly gentleman who, over sixty, was living with his third wife. She was in her early thirties and had borne him a son and a daughter. The first wife would come to visit, chatting amicably with the third wife, showing sisterly affection without a shred of jealousy. The first wife, herself in her sixties, told me she had taken up Buddhism and was no longer interested in sex, and it was just as well for the old man to find it elsewhere in the family, rather than outside the home.

I gathered the old man was not as interested in having a younger wife for sex as in her bearing him another son to carry on his name. However, I suspected things were not always harmonious in their household when one day the third wife showed up at our house with her two young children. She asked for temporary shelter, for she was planning to elope; somehow she had found my address and decided to take a chance with the first outsider who had entered her closely controlled family environment, though we were really strangers. Shocked and concerned, I had little advice for her, being a child myself, except to turn to my parents for help. My parents were torn between protecting her and feeling obligated to notify her husband. Luckily for all of us, she had left enough clues for her husband to trace her and take her home. After the storm was over I had the occasion to discuss this episode with the elderly gentleman. He was totally baffled about why his third wife, who seemed to have all the material comforts and his undivided attention for their son, would choose to leave him. He even showed me the large bank account and real estate holdings he had accumulated on behalf of this son borne by the third wife. Little did he understand the stirrings of discontent in a woman in such a repressed environment.

Before Liberation it was always assumed that a man was free to choose more than one wife. In Taiwan, the ambiguous attempt to discourage polygamy by limiting formal legal status and legal rights to the first wife only did not deter men from continuing to bring other women into the household. One of my high school classmates, a girl from a prominent literary Taiwanese family, lived with her traditional father, who had three wives: the first legal wife who was the mother of my classmate; the second wife, originally their chambermaid, whose plain looks made it apparent that her sole function in the household continued to be serving the others; and the third wife, a sexy, flamboyant woman who had been a leading singer of Chinese opera. Despite her standing as the legal wife, my friend's mother was often in silent pain. I visited her house often and was struck by the emotional trauma inevitably created by such an arrangement.

After the death of her husband a woman's life might become even more unpleasant. Widowhood was accepted only if the widow never married again. Local communities would set up monuments for widows who remained chaste until they died. In old China it was considered better still if a wife died along with her husband, by committing suicide. Although probably very rare, this was the saintly and noble ideal for the loyal bereaved wife. A widower, on the other hand, was expected to marry again, and the sooner the better. He needed a woman to run his household and look after his children. None of the widows that I personally knew ever remarried—my first aunt, Grandmother Li, my mother-in-law, and several other aunts, all of whom became widows at a relatively young age.

It was always a mystery to me what a married woman did to meet her own needs. Given the total cultural taboo against any interest in men other than her husband, there was little opportunity for a woman to wander too far. Should infidelity be committed, a married woman could be stoned to death in certain communities. It was also grounds for termination of the marriage contract, disgracing the woman's family forever. Not that Chinese women never developed any extra-marital relationships—they did so in utter secrecy and in constant fear of discovery. The husband whose wife had wandered was usually described as "wearing a green hat"; becoming a cuckold.

Since Liberation the status of married women has changed profoundly, both in the mainland and elsewhere. Chinese views on marriage have, however, remained doggedly practical. During the Cultural Revolution my cousin Zhenli married a man with a "pure ideology" and a farm background, both considered good standards for choosing a marriage partner at that time. She married without developing any preliminary bond with her future husband, having just broken off her long-standing relationship with a man whose political background was considered questionable. Years later, after the end of the Cultural Revolution, Zhenli ran into her former boyfriend again. Both were now working in the same city.

Zhenli recalled her own mixed emotions upon seeing her friend who by now was also married and successful in his occupation. Zhenli told me she had a sense of regret that she had allowed the political pressures of the times dictate her own choice of a marriage partner.

"Knowing what you know now," I asked, "would you have done anything differently?"

Zhenli looked at me quizzically. "Probably not," she sighed. "You don't really expect a Chinese to ignore the practical side of marriage, do you?"

I said nothing. Then Zhenli added, "You know romance has nothing to do with marriage."

5

A Departure from the Norm— Sixth Aunt

My cousin Zhenli, daughter of my sixth uncle and aunt, was born six months after her parents' wedding, an uncomfortable fact that was to be a shrouded secret in the family. Grandmother Li and Mother went so far as to suspect, with feelings of resentment toward Sixth Aunt, that Sixth Uncle might not be Zhenli's father. The issue would never be resolved, for Sixth Uncle, an air force pilot fighting the Japanese, died in a plane crash before Zhenli was born, and Sixth Aunt ran off with another man a few months after she was born.

I constantly heard tales of my Sixth Aunt, Lingling, while growing up. From all accounts, the Li family considered her the beautiful and hateful witch who had captured the heart of their only male heir and had destroyed his life. After a long weekend leave at home with Sixth Aunt who was having an uncomfortable pregnancy and demanding his constant attention, he was shot down in his plane. Many years later I could still hear Mother saying, "I couldn't see how anyone could have been alert enough to fly into the war zone after staying up all night looking after that witch." At other times she would express reluctant admiration of how Sixth Aunt could have any man falling under her feet, even in the most incredible state. She would tell me and Zhenli that when Sixth Aunt was in the hospital waiting to give birth to Zhenli, Mother visited her with a basket of fruit, only to find her propped up in bed, being tenderly and gallantly fed a pear, newly sliced by a young man. Love and yearning in his eyes, he did not even notice Mother's coming into the room. Mother recalled her sense of wonder, mixed with envy and anger, at this scene. "Lingling could command such devotion from a total stranger, even when she was about to go into the delivery room!"

Sixth Aunt Lingling was only five feet two, slight and delicate. She had a perfectly oval face with big round eyes that seemed to come alive even in a still photo. Her mouth was full and sensual, turned up at the corners as she looked at you. At age sixteen, when she met my uncle, she had already led a precocious life. Born into a prominent political family—her father was a county executive—she left home early, after her mother had died and her father had remarried, this time to a much younger woman. Lingling went to Shanghai to pursue her dream of becoming an actress. There her quick wit and charm easily won her a small place in a theater company. She began to travel extensively across the country with the theater group.

When Sixth Uncle met her, she had the reputation of being the darling of the air force. She was easily the most sought-after date for the young pilots away from home. Sixth Uncle fell madly in love. His serious interest in Lingling did not please his family at home, but he dealt with the opposition quietly and stubbornly. In one of his letters to his family during the turbulent romance with Lingling, he wrote:

> I received your letter today. Knowing what you would have to say about my unacceptable life, I have put it aside, determined not to read it until tomorrow. For tonight I'm taking Lingling out to dinner, and I do not need any distraction from enjoying her company.

As I was reading this passage, and many similar letters to his family, I could sense the struggle Sixth Uncle must have gone through by marrying her when all odds were against the marriage. But it was quite in character for him to have things his way. His family never fully approved his entering the air force, for example, but Sixth Uncle joined anyway. When the Sino-Japanese war began, Sixth Uncle was a patriotic and red-blooded young man, ready for the fight. Sensing his family's disapproval—no sole male heir should be allowed to risk his life on the battlefield and endanger the family bloodline—he secretly enlisted as a combat pilot. A few days before he was to report to the air base, he announced his new career to a shocked family. Grandmother Li was tearful, but to everyone's surprise she gave him the support he needed, for as fearful as she was, she was equally committed to fighting the Japanese war. His sisters had a harder time accepting his decision, their own concern for him compounded by their fears that if anything happened to him, Grandmother Li would be inconsolable.

I had never met Sixth Uncle, but judging from numerous photos in the family album kept by Mother, he was slim and tall, handsome in a gentle, delicate way. His features —slightly slanted eyes, long and expressive face, high nose bridge, a small, regular mouth—seemed more those of an artist than a combat air force pilot. Artistic, he played the violin well, and was also one of the top students in his class. Sixth Uncle was also shy, romantic, and not always lucky in love.

Before he met Lingling, he had long had a secret crush on Mother's closest girlfriend. A few years his senior, she was a smart, beautiful girl from a wealthy family. For whatever reasons, he never revealed his passion to the girl despite the fact that those around him, including the girl herself, were aware of his feelings for her. In one of his letters to my mother, written from the air base, he explained himself:

> I probably will never confess my love to her, but nothing shall stop me from feeling the way I do. She is simply too good for me, too much beyond my reach. I ask myself: What can I bring her? She has everything —education, looks, character. All I have is an aborted schooling and a risky career. No, I shall carry my secret to the grave.

Away from home, he could no longer stay in touch with his secret love. For a while nothing happened. Then my mother heard about Sixth Uncle's interest in Lingling.

Sixth Uncle's secret love for this girl was always a tantalizing story for me. Unfortunately, Mother kept no photos of her, only her own incomplete descriptions of a girl who must have been extraordinary. My curiosity, however, was finally satisfied in 1982 when I returned to China for the second time. Typical of life's coincidences, I was driven from the airport in a van arranged for by the institute in Wuhan (my mother's birthplace) where I would be lecturing that summer. Two young men from the Office of Foreign Affairs escorted me and the group of visiting scholars. During the drive, one of the young men turned to me and suddenly asked whether I was the daughter of my mother, calling her by her maiden name, and whether I knew my mother's closest friend, who happened to be his mother. Evidently he had looked up my profile (kept by the sponsoring agency) and found the connection. I had been given a key to the past.

As soon as I had settled into the guest house, I proceeded to make arrangements to meet this mystery lady, who was in fact still living in the same city, now a retired English teacher. Unexpectedly, she dropped in to see me one afternoon just as I returned from the classroom. Our meeting seemed to shatter all the fantasies I had formed about this mysterious lady. Over sixty, she appeared old, worn, plain. Her hair, almost entirely gray, was straight, with a shoulder-length blunt cut. Big black-rimmed glasses took up half of her small, nondescript face. Her face was completely wrinkled, with a sallow complexion—with little trace of past beauty. She walked with a rather strange gait.

She became my regular visitor for the next two weeks, and as we continued to see each other, her sensibility and spirit gradually began to emerge. I now saw a woman still beautiful, and full of vibrant spirit and life. The day before I left Wuhan, she showed me an old photo of herself, taken long ago when she was young. "I gave the same photo to your sixth uncle many years ago," she said as she handed me the picture somewhat shyly, as a parting souvenir. I saw a comely young girl, dressed in fashionable attire, sitting on the grass with an open, engaging smile, eyes full of dreams and hope. She could melt any man's heart. I finally understood my sixth uncle's secret love.

If my sixth uncle's secret love had been for the challenge of quiet intelligence, his love for my sixth aunt would be for the sensual and physical, the stormy and passionate. Sixth Aunt moved with a fluid sensuality, and every gesture and expression meant one thing: Notice me, I am the most desirable woman alive. And people, men and women, did notice her wherever she was, whenever she walked by. Unlike the subtle suggestion of romantic interest by Sixth Uncle's secret love, Sixth Aunt was daring in her ardent pursuit of him. The story was that Sixth Aunt, for reasons unknown to the people around her, including my sixth uncle, simply had made up her mind that Sixth Uncle was to be her next conquest. Mother described in disgust the time Sixth Aunt pleaded having no transportation to get back to her apartment in town after a night out with Sixth Uncle and ended up spending the night in the air force barracks. Sixth Uncle and his fellow airmen had to smuggle her in, for it was quite irregular and improper and violated the base rule.

Had she tried, Sixth Aunt probably could have succeeded in becoming a serious actress, but it was obvious that her life goal lay elsewhere. It was as if she had found the secret of her survival: capturing men who would support her needs. She devoted her full attention to ways of winning affection from others. Yet, try as she would, she did not succeed with Sixth Uncle's family. Finding her alien to their Muslim tradition and unladylike by traditional Chinese standards, Grandmother Li and her five daughters were determined to dislike Sixth Aunt from the start. No amount of artful manipulation by Sixth Aunt could convince them otherwise. However, singly and as a group, they cared about Sixth Uncle's happiness and began to waver as he remained loyal and persistent in his love for Lingling. Sixth Uncle's stubbornness, I gather, was in part assisted by another part of the code of conduct in this family of women—that a woman should obey three males in her life: her father, her husband, and her son. There was a limit to Grandmother Li's persuasive power when it came to her favorite son's wishes. So Sixth Uncle and Lingling had a wedding at last.

Mother told me that the mourning and tension in the family after Sixth Uncle's death was intense and unbearable. Their antipathy exacerbated by deep grief, the family blamed Sixth Aunt for the death of the beloved male heir of the family. If only Sixth Uncle had not returned home on leave to care for his demanding wife, they reasoned, he would not have been shot down by the enemy plane. No one seemed to have paid much attention to Sixth Aunt's own loss. If not for the imminent birth of Zhenli, Sixth Aunt could have fared even worse in the role of the "evil woman" who had cast a spell on and brought down her young husband. Years later, when Zhenli finally located her mother and discussed this period in Sixth Aunt's life, she confirmed that from Sixth Aunt's perspective, the family had treated her most unfairly. Receiving little sympathy and support from her husband's family, she began to seek male companionship, and had no problem finding it. Men flocked around her, flattered to receive her attention. Male visitors knocked on the door, and Mother, outspoken and hot-tempered, would turn them away. "See her anywhere but here," she would exclaim, slamming the door on them, "This is my house!" Undaunted, they kept coming back, and Sixth Aunt kept going out with them. The night before her delivery, she had been out dancing until dawn, much to the chagrin of the Li family.

It therefore came as no surprise to anyone that Sixth Aunt would not stay long after the birth of Zhenli. Barely seventeen, she was full of her own plans. One afternoon, she left with a mysterious male friend and never returned.

Zhenli would grow up in Grandmother's house with me,

and later, with First Aunt, following Grandmother's death, when Father returned from abroad to take Mother and me to Taiwan. Zhenli was curious about her natural mother, this unconventional, rebellious woman whom she had never known. In 1978, after I had made an initial contact with Zhenli from the United States, she spoke of her "mother-hunt." Now established as a government official and living in Beijing, Zhenli was at last able to use her formal and informal contacts to track down her mother.

Making numerous inquiries through Sixth Uncle's old comrades in the war, Zhenli had finally succeeded in locating my sixth aunt through a mutual acquaintance. I was in Beijing in the summer of 1985 with a New York State delegation when Zhenli excitedly told me of her search. "For years I thought about her. I wanted to understand why she had left me in the care of others. I wanted to know more about her life with my father, and with all the others after she left me," Zhenli said, tears in her eyes. "I couldn't believe that she married four times. Four times!"

Zhenli arranged to meet with her mother. The first meeting was traumatic for both of them. With guilt and remorse, Sixth Aunt embraced Zhenli, who, perplexed by her own lack of emotional response, did not find herself moved by the stranger's tears. Sixth Aunt's aging and her less-than-peaceful existence during the last three decades had left her no longer the beauty who once bewitched every man who met her. She seemed fatigued and weather-beaten; a lifelong battle to survive as a love object had taken its toll. But she remained erect in her posture, the same self-reliant attitude about life intact, and one could still see traces of the old magic in her.

Sixth Aunt told Zhenli that the adverse climate in the Li household had driven her out, that indeed she had gone off with another dashing air force pilot, a friend of Sixth Uncle's, only to become a widow for the second time. He too had been killed in the war. Determined to find more stability in life, she married again, this time to an architect, with whom she bore two children. Her third husband, though dependable in many ways, was physically abusive to her, and Sixth Aunt took action again. Not wanting to be a battered wife, she divorced him and left him with the children. This time she was more careful in her search for a mate, and found a renowned engineer who had recently become a widower. Though in her forties by then, Sixth Aunt had not lost her charm. She again became the pursuer. Though separated by several provinces after his transfer during the Cultural Revolution, the engineer was warmed by her attention and finally proposed marriage. Two more children were born of this union. This last marriage survived. Now Sixth Aunt, in her sixties, appeared to have mellowed with her late-found domestic bliss.

Having bottled up years of feeling abandoned, Zhenli found it difficult to accept her mother's pattern of life. Zhenli and I had the same conversation over and over:

Zhenli: I don't see why she would leave me.

  I: What choice did she have? She had no means of self-support. The Li family couldn't stand her. Besides, she was young, she had to live again.

Zhenli: But why did she have to marry again and again? Good women stay with their marriages, no matter how miserable.

  I: Give her credit for walking out of a bad marriage. How many women in her generation dared to?

Zhenli: She was obviously not a good mother. Look at

what she did to me. She abandoned her other
children too.

I: I won't defend her there. But many women cannot be good mothers. Perhaps your mother
should not have tried motherhood.

Zhenli: I still cannot forgive her for what she did to me.

I: I can't blame you for feeling the way you do,
and it's difficult to look at things her way. I only
ask: What would we have done in her position
three decades ago?

Zhenli's search for her mother had troubled her fourth
aunt, my mother, whose feelings of resentment toward
this fascinating woman remain strong to this day.
Mother heard about Zhenli's mother-hunt and considered it a wasted effort and indeed a betrayal of the Li
family. I tried to get Mother to understand the natural
emotion of anyone toward a biological parent. But I
could not convince her that Zhenli, independent of the
family's feeling about Sixth Aunt, had a right to find
answers for herself.

Racked by her own reaction to her mother, and feeling
disloyal to my mother's family, Zhenli reached her own
conclusions about her mother: "I don't think she ever
cared for me. It was difficult at first to accept, but now
I don't even care."

One year after mother and daughter had been reunited, Sixth Aunt, who now lived in another province,
visited Zhenli in Beijing. Finding very little to discuss
with her daughter, Sixth Aunt cut short her visit and left
after spending only one night in Zhenli's apartment.

Curiously, Zhenli found herself becoming close to
Sixth Aunt's present husband, a mature, understanding
man who seemed genuinely fond of Sixth Aunt. Zhenli

also befriended one of Sixth Aunt's other daughters, dying of cancer in the hospital. Zhenli visited the daughter many times; they shared their thoughts, each different, of their mother.

I knew it would take a long, long time, if not the rest of a lifetime, for Zhenli to find peace with her own past, and with her mother's. I knew it would not be possible for her, for Mother, or for any of the Li family, to be forgiving toward my sixth aunt. But perhaps it is easier for me, a semi-outsider, a generation apart, to see the larger picture of my Sixth Aunt's situation: a lone young woman in a hostile world, a man's world, surrounded by cultural taboos and prohibitions. She had defied the norm and had survived longer than many, and possibly in a way, more successfully than most. But she was still the product of her time and culture—a willing victim, but a victim just the same.

And in my own way, having lived with the conflicting values of East and West, I can afford to be a bit more understanding. I know when I visit China again, I will sit down with Sixth Aunt and try to understand her life from another perspective.

CHAPTER

6

First Uncle— Father's Idol

Father did not often talk about his side of the family. On the rare occasions when he did, his eldest brother, First Uncle, was prominently featured, usually in connection with lessons about growing up, good work habits and all the sturdy characteristics a good man should possess. We, my two younger brothers and I, came to expect that everything connected with First Uncle was noble and good.

I never met my eldest uncle. He died far away, after a long battle with tuberculosis and accompanying cataracts in his eyes and severe psoriasis. His death came in 1945, toward the end of the Sino-Japanese War. I knew that he had picked my name, Murong, which means "remembering Chengdu city," my birthplace; taken separately, Rong also means "lotus flower." First Uncle had been asked by my parents to name me, a deferential gesture generally made to the head of the family. And First Uncle had indeed been the head of the Pu family for many years. In fact, First Uncle seemed to be the real father to my own father, and to all of his other younger brothers and sister.

55

Father came from a poor, impoverished Hakka family, non-Muslim by tradition, in a small village in Guangdong province. Hakka means "visiting family," a term applied in the south to a group of Chinese who had migrated from the north in the Tang dynasty. Grandfather Pu had operated a freighter boat for a living, while Grandmother Pu tended vegetable fields to supplement the family income. The Hakka men and women were known for their physical stamina and diligent work habits. The Hakka women were free of the custom of foot-binding, unlike women in other parts of China. Economic necessity made their labor essential. The prevailing beauty standard of three-inch-golden-lotus feet, a common description of the small, dainty bound feet, meant little to Grandmother Pu and all the other women in her village. Carrying a full load as equal partners to the men, these women worked outside as well as inside the home.

I doubt whether Grandfather or Grandmother Pu ever went to school long enough to acquire a basic education. I met Grandmother Pu several times. Even at a young age, I was struck by her peasant ways. Good-hearted and robust, Grandmother Pu never paid much attention to table manners. She would adjust her dentures during a meal, in front of everyone. What also impressed me was how Father, genteel and educated, was totally accepting of her. Never critical nor appearing embarrassed, Father was his mother's loyal, dutiful son. Father probably modelled himself after his eldest brother, the man who had set the highest standard of filial responsibility.

First Uncle was in middle school when Grandfather Pu died in a boat accident. Left with no resources but the vegetable fields, Grandmother Pu relied on a distant relative to help support her and her children. First Uncle went right to work, taking odd jobs after school to lessen the family's financial burden. He would work late each night in his uncle's store, and write for newspapers to earn extra income. In addition, he took care of his younger brothers and sister. On top of all this, First Uncle was the chief editor of the school paper and president of the school's student association.

Unfortunately, poor nutrition and heavy work would later take their toll. First Uncle began to have recurring health problems, eventually diagnosed as tuberculosis, a lingering illness that would in the end claim his life.

From physical appearances, First Uncle showed no signs of frail health. Of medium height and weight, he looked like a sturdy, healthy intellectual. Always well-groomed and well-dressed, particularly in later years when he had the means to do so, he appeared unruffled and in control. Father physically resembled First Uncle and the resemblance did not stop there. For example the closeness of their brush-writing style was quite astonishing.

I discovered First Uncle's brush-writing style by reading his poetry books, left to Father as remembrances. Later, in 1968, when Father and friends of First Uncle decided to commemorate First Uncle's contribution to the publishing and educational field by publishing his diary, I had the opportunity to see his original handwriting. His diary, kept between 1941 and 1945—the final years of his life—described only one part of his life. My knowledge about him was broadened by reading the articles about him published as appendices to the diary.

I learned, for example, that First Uncle had had no adult male role model at home while growing up. His inner drive to excel seemed to have received no particular reinforcement from his family, but came from the call of a higher order in charting his life course. Yet he had his feet firmly on the ground. Every step he took helped his family; all his activities had direct benefits for others.

After struggling to finish his middle school education and then go on to get his college degree despite meager family resources, he took a newspaper job. Before long he had a stable, if not prosperous, livelihood. He wasted no time in lending a helping hand to his younger brothers and sister who naturally followed in his footsteps to complete their educations as well.

Father, the third of the four brothers, went to college in Shanghai solely on financial support from First Uncle. Father recalled the weekends he spent at First Uncle's garden residence in Shanghai and his exposure to First Uncle's publishing and political world. First Uncle had become an important figure in the Guomindang party, the ruling party of the Nationalist government. Father derived more than financial support from his elder brother; he would consult First Uncle on all major decisions in his life.

My second uncle, on the other hand, was a disappointment for First Uncle. Though smart and accomplished, upon the completion of his medical education Second Uncle tried vary hard to distance himself from the rest of the family. It was as if, having lived in the shadow of First Uncle all his youth, he could not wait to be free of that influence and of family responsibilities. In one of the entries in his diary, First Uncle wrote:

I have not seen my second brother for weeks now. I had asked him to send some money to our sister back home to help her purchase books and supplies for school, but knowing him, I doubt he has done it. Only today my landlady mentioned to me casually that she had seen my second brother at the teahouse in town every day during the last two weeks, drinking and dining with his friends. Will I ever convince him of his duty to the family?

Forever worried about his family, and later about the middle school he had established, First Uncle had no time for romance. But romantic love did not neglect him. He would have many devoted female companions all his life, despite his confirmed bachelorhood. One of his women friends, the one he was seeing before he died, exemplified what First Uncle must have found in women he associated with. She was as loyal and as committed to the same causes as he was. The fact that First Uncle did not seem interested in marriage (he once confessed to his family that his poor physical health would always prevent his marrying) did not discourage her. Her devotion to him never wavered, even during the last years when he suffered a series of setbacks. In his diary, during the time he was suffering extreme physical pain from recurrent bouts of influenza, cataracts, and skin lesions that would not heal, he wrote of her visit to his country home:

> Today Fuchuan came to see me with a basket of fruit and a live hen, after walking ten miles to get here. She also brought me some herbal medicine for my hands and feet, for all of my extremities hurt from broken and infected blisters that will not heal. As soon as she walked in, she rushed to the kitchen to prepare the medicine. I was too weak to follow, so I watched her back, tears clouding my vision. I marvel at this woman: What makes her do what she does?

Again and again in his diary, First Uncle would write about her frequent and welcome visits, until he stopped writing altogether. One entry described her offer to send money to First Uncle's sister at home, after learning that Second Uncle had failed again to make the necessary payments. She had become practically part of the Pu family, as devoted and loyal as First Uncle.

His deteriorating health notwithstanding, First Uncle never gave up hope. He would write about new plans for the school and his newspaper after the war. Unfortunately, he had to face another tragic event during those difficult times: the loss of his fourth brother, an air force pilot in the Sino-Japanese War. When the report of Fourth Uncle's being missing in action reached him, First Uncle was at a low point in his illness. Grief-stricken, but not wanting to upset his ailing mother at home, he kept the news from the family for some time. Father, too, was kept in the dark for months. When he finally learned the news, he wrote to First Uncle from the United States:

> I know how you must have felt. If it means anything to you, you should be proud of the important role you have played in our much-loved brother's life. He died a hero to his country and a tribute to his family. Let's plan on setting up a special scholarship in his name in your school after the war. I should be returning home by then.

First Uncle spent most of the period of his illness growing a vegetable garden. The landlady, a peasant women herself, teased First Uncle about his attempt at physical labor, for he seemed to her too much an intellectual to be much good in the garden. First Uncle told her that his own mother had done this for a living and that as a youngster he had been familiar with such physical labor.

Doing his own shopping was both a necessity and a way of alleviating the boredom of living alone. First Uncle wrote long meticulous accounts of the inflation in the prices of food and household items. He remained honest and caring throughout, sharing his meager food supply with those in need as supplies diminished during the war. On one occasion a meat merchant undercharged him. When he discovered the error after returning home First Uncle went back to return the money, taking the merchant completely by surprise. During the difficult war years many abandoned the normal peacetime social order, particularly in the more deprived areas.

Until he passed away, First Uncle remained in touch with Father. He also showed a keen interest in Mother's life and in my own growing up, far away in Chengdu. Mother showed high regard for First Uncle's opinion. She would also act as the intermediary for Father, who usually sent in the same envelope his letters to her and to his brother.

First Uncle died without seeing his aging mother again, or my father, his third brother, or his other brothers and sister. His funeral was arranged by nearby friends as First Uncle was in a remote Sichuan village far from any close relatives when he died. He left his estate to the middle school he had built and left his personal mementos to his brothers and sister. Father got First Uncle's diary and books of poetry. I wonder if his woman friend saved anything for herself. I hope so, but she probably had memories enough of First Uncle. She was most likely with him before he died, for she alone of his friends had watched his deteriorating condition. I wonder what happened to her afterward. Somehow I think she would have moved on to other interests in life. That was what First Uncle would have wanted.

First Uncle's sacrifices were obvious to others, his happiness known only to himself. Perhaps First Uncle was happiest when he was helpful to others. He fulfilled the role expected of him socially and culturally. Along with his superior status in the Chinese family, the eldest son must bear a heavier burden than other family members. Both family and society expect this loyalty and sacrifice. It is not unusual for the eldest son in China to contribute to the welfare of the rest of the family, but it is not always customary for the eldest to extend his concern beyond the family. Most Chinese families remain close-knit, self-centered, even selfish units. First Uncle's sense of social obligation extended far beyond his family. His personal encouragement of the students who enter his school free of charge was his special and precious contribution to society. First Uncle exemplified the best of the traditional Chinese ideal of social duty.

Perhaps I see him most clearly in his influence on my father, his third brother, the only sibling who has had a life outside China. A few years ago, after Father had made contact with his own family in Guangzhou, composed now of only his sister and her family, Father started to send money back home. He sent it to the same Hakka village where he was born, thus completing the cycle of mutual assistance my first uncle had so ably begun many years ago.

And I remain grateful to this man—for giving me my name, for being a member of my family.

I Become a Boy—
The Exodus of 1949

P eople were everywhere. And the baggage—all different shapes, sizes, and colors—bundles and boxes,
wrapped in bed sheets or blankets. I had never seen such
a crowd, all cramming into the warehouse by the dockside
waiting for the vessel to arrive at Nanjing harbor—except
that the ship was delayed once more. I was told we had
no choice that night but to sleep on the concrete floor in
the warehouse, for we must try to get on the ship first thing
in the morning.

Mother was trying to get me and my infant brother
Muming, barely one month old, out of Nanjing in the
winter of 1948. We were going to Wuhan first, before joining Father, who had gone ahead of us to join the Nationalist
government on Taiwan, off the southeast coast of China.
Luckily my cousin, Lianfeng, an army officer in the Nationalist Army who was planning to rejoin his own outfit in
Sichuan shortly, was on hand to deal with the crowd. He
carried me over his head through the crowd to find a few

square feet so we could set up our bedding on the floor for the night. I followed, half-dazed and half-amused, intrigued by the people in the warehouse, people who were dressed differently from us and spoke many different dialects. When we found a spot, a woman caught my immediate attention. She was taking a piece of dark, dry bread out of the inside pocket of her cotton-padded jacket, her fingernails long and dark. She had with her a small girl about my age, who by then seemed more interested in the baby doll I was clutching than the piece of bread her mother was handing her.

My mother whispered to me that they probably had come from Henan province in northern China, a province that was known for its poverty and seasonal famine.

It was getting dark outside. Candles were lit inside the warehouse, interspersed with old-fashioned oil lamps. I lay down. After tucking me into the heavy yellow-and-brown-striped woolen blanket that Father had brought home from the United States, Mother went to attend to my brother. Distracted by the noise in the warehouse, I looked around and saw out of the corner of my eye that the Henan family was getting ready to settle down next to us. With no bedding or blankets, they seemed prepared to sleep in the clothes they had on. I was appalled. I turned to Mother and asked if I could lend my blanket to the Henan family. Mother looked at them and said yes. The Henan women, smiling with appreciation, took the blanket from me to cover her daughter, as I snuggled over to Mother's side to keep warm.

At dawn we were all in motion, for the ship had finally arrived. Agile cousin Lianfeng navigated us through the crowds to get us on board. I lost sight of the Henan family after they returned the blanket to us, but there were plenty of travelers crowded around us to capture my attention. In the commotion of passengers struggling to get on the ship, I was left alone for a while as Mother supervised the transfer of our luggage. Finally, Lianfeng got on as well, to escort us to Wuhan.

Mother had wanted to visit her own family in Wuhan before leaving for Taiwan. And she was comforted by the thought that, once home, her mother and her elder sisters would know exactly how to care for my infant brother, as I had been taken care of by Mother's eldest sister, my first aunt, during infancy, when Mother was somewhat overwhelmed by the task of being a "new" mother. She was also developing a bad head cold from sleeping on the concrete floor the night before. Little did she know that I would bring worse to the Li family. I got a full head of lice from sharing my blanket with the Henan girl. By the time the ship reached Wuhan, my head lice were a critical problem.

Muslim families are meticulous in their living conditions and personal hygiene and are not experienced in treating head lice. My condition completely baffled them. First, they tried some ready-made solution from the drugstore, then they tried giving me a hair permanent at the beauty salon, hoping to kill or chase away the lice under the extreme heat. This resulted in an hysterical scene in the beauty shop. The hairdresser, upon seeing crawling insects in my scalp, dropped everything and ran out of the shop. Finally they came up with a solution: I should have my long hair cut short, like a boy.

I was to be a boy until after we landed in Taiwan. An entirely new wardrobe was put together for me with boy's shirts, overalls, and pants. Gone were my floral prints and skirts; now I wore solid colors. I went along with the transformation and thought, when I looked at myself in the mirror, that I could easily pass as a boy. The fact that I couldn't wear girls clothes for a while did not bother me. This final strategy did work, for the lice were gradually gone, speeded up by use of more lotion from the drugstore.

Our stay in Grandmother Li's house in Wuhan was short and hectic. As the Chinese New Year was approaching, the women of the house had begun the holiday preparations. Shopping and endless cooking would fill the days. The political situation, as unstable as it was, did not seem to have much impact on how Chinese celebrated their holidays. "Dynasties come and go" was the common attitude, even though the founding of the Republic of China in 1911 had made dynasties anachronistic. Our household seemed indifferent to the gathering victories of the Communist Revolution from which we were about to flee.

In the social structure of the old China to which we belonged, women seldom discussed politics or ideology. Isolated by status and privilege, the women of our family comprehended little of the momentous forces that Mao Zedong and the Chinese Communist Party were leading against the armies of Chiang Kai-shek. We were quite unaware of the historical significance of the long struggle against the exploitation and impoverishment of the Chinese people, both in the cities and in the countryside. Even if it had been explained to us, we would not have understood the profound resentment and outrage that had accumulated among the Chinese people. Nor would we women have understood the complex mixture of fear and indignation that must have been tormenting the minds of our fathers and husbands.

We never questioned father's high position in the Nationalist Air Force, nor his unswerving loyalty to Chiang Kai-shek.

Like most of those who were preparing to follow Chiang Kai-shek to Taiwan in 1949, Mother thought that our exile would be brief, that we would be able to come home again soon, within a few months at most. She became immersed in the holiday activities with her sisters and relatives.

One night, after we had washed and put away the dinner dishes and Grandmother Li was getting ready for her evening ritual of unwrapping the bindings on her tiny deformed feet, we heard a loud pounding on our front door, followed by urgent shouts of "Open the door, open the door!" Since our front door was some distance from the back rooms where Grandmother Li and I were staying, we dropped everything to rush toward the door. It was my first aunt's voice. She had gone out shopping that evening with Mother and Second Aunt. I immediately loosened the latch on the front door to let them in. All three rushed in, puffing and panting, and quickly closed the door behind them. Grandmother burst out, "Bless the Lord! Your faces are as white as sheets. What happened?"

Mother said they had been robbed, all three of them, in the alley leading to the house. A young man, in his twenties, was interested not only in their cash, but also in the jewelry they were wearing. Second Aunt interjected, "It was a good thing I was too fast for him. I put the bag of yarn I had just bought over my hand to hide my rings." After surrendering their money and jewelry (except for Second Aunt's rings), they ran to the house as fast as they could. With the story told and nerves calmed by cups of hot tea, the question came up as to whether this incident should be reported. First Aunt said, "What for? The police these days have no interest in solving crimes. All they want to do is leave town as fast as they can." Like other officials working for the Guomindang government, police officers were attempting to flee to Taiwan. Mother and Second Aunt felt strongly that the robbery should be reported to the local authorities, and First Aunt gave in. Nothing ever came of it, of course.

I remember that New Year celebration. All of Mother's sisters were home for the holidays, including Third Aunt, who had married a wealthy landowner in a faraway county, and Fifth Aunt, who had married the police chief of Hankou (a part of Wuhan) in Hubei. Third Aunt came with a truckload of food from her country estate, her freshly ground cornmeal the most welcome of all. Third Aunt had already acquired the local dialect of the place where she now lived, and all her sisters teased her about it. My fifth aunt, the most educated (the only one ever to attend college) and the most compliant (she had been treated as the baby by all her sisters), came home with her imposing police-chief husband, her chauffeur, and her beautifully wrapped presents.

Zhenli and I loved to visit Fifth Aunt in Hankou, nearby. Her residence, built in Western style, was complete with two Indian guards who wore red headdresses and black beards. I had not seen men with beards before, and was fascinated by the long, curly beards on these two guards, who spoke good Mandarin Chinese and were very friendly toward us. My fifth uncle wielded tremendous power in the criminal justice system in Hankou, and 1948 seemed to be a busy year for him. Arrests had increased as well as the number of executions. The loose use of capital punishment was common; with no due process, many petty crimes resulted in execution. Fifth Uncle seemed unmoved at all by this, treating the increase in crime as a natural consequence of political and social unrest. I never had the nerve to watch him in action. My fifth uncle had an air about him that did not make little girls like Zhenli and me warm up to him. Later, after we had moved to Taiwan, we learned that he had been arrested and put in jail by the Communists, for reasons unknown, and that he had died of an illness while in prison.

My aunts now cooked for days to get ready for the New Year's feast. For the ten-fragrant-vegetable dish, days were spent cutting, slicing, and drying the vegetables in the sun before the final cooking. A popular New Year's snack for the Muslim family was a doughnut-like fried dough cooked in vegetable oil and kept as a favorite morning snack. Beef was featured on the menu, with every conceivable way of cooking, preserving, and serving it, as the Muslims do not eat pork. Zhenli and I were having a great time.

Beneath the happy celebration was a sense of sadness that the family would be separated for a while. Grandmother Li was sullen and quiet for she inevitably remembered her dead son, my sixth uncle, during the holiday season. I caught Mother and her sisters shedding tears together. They did not know that this would be the last time they would all be together.

The day we were to leave for Guangzhou by train to catch the passenger ship for Taiwan, it was snowing hard outside. I was awakened by Mother and was rushed to get dressed for the waiting car. Grandmother was too distraught to get up from her bed. I heard a commotion in her room—Mother and her sisters were hovering over her to comfort her. My orphaned cousin Zhenli was still in bed, as she was not going to Taiwan with us, but she was wide-awake and wanted to come with us. I heard Mother trying to soothe her while Grandmother was telling her she could not go. Zhenli was crying. Then it was all over and we were escorted out of the house, headed for the railroad. Mother had with her boxes of cooked dishes, enough to feed ten people, and once again Lianfeng accompanied us, all the way to Guangzhou.

At the Guangzhou train station, we were met by Father's sister, as we were going to stay at the residence for single teachers of the middle school where my aunt was teaching. My aunt, meeting me for the first time, was curious about my boyish get-up, but assumed that it was done for the convenience of travel.

Our first evening meal was Cantonese. I ate pea pods for the first time and thought they tasted rather strange. But the Cantonese desserts were delicious and plentiful. Mother settled down for the time being, waiting for the confirmation of her ship's schedule and Father's arrival —Father had decided to pick us up at Guangzhou.

I got to know my aunt's teaching colleagues well. But I sensed Mother was not entirely comfortable in Guangzhou. She complained about the inflation in food prices and the expectation that she should foot the entire food bill for the teachers in the residence—all of us ate together at one round table—since all the teachers seemed to be in a perpetual state of poverty. At the dinner table there was the usual discussion about the political situation. The general sentiment was that the Nationalist armies would lose sooner or later from their sheer absence of will to fight and from the internal corruption. I listened, only half understanding the discussion. When the conversation got beyond me I went to see the cook and her son in the shanty next to the residence, and I would watch her do her daily chores as calmly and methodically as ever. I would be somewhat assured that nothing horrible could happen to her and her son, or to the people of this land, for all they wanted was to lead a simple life.

It was clear that the adults' fears for the future of the nation aside, few thought that going to Taiwan would be the answer. My aunt's colleagues warned me about the potentially harsh living conditions on the island of Taiwan. "We've heard that people there sleep in the open air and have no clothes on," they would say, "and the food—they have nothing to eat except bananas." Mother tried to ignore their comments but could not shake off her own uncertainty about life in Taiwan.

Father finally arrived, healthy and stronger. He mentioned the warmer climate in Taiwan and advised Mother not to worry too much about winter clothing. This time I was glad to leave; my aunt's place in Guangzhou had run out of charm for me.

The sea journey to Taiwan was long and arduous. Crossing the South China Sea was no easy voyage, unlike the river trip by water we had taken to get out of Nanjing. Now all of us became very seasick. I remember throwing up numerous times, in the cabin, out of the cabin, everywhere I turned. My infant brother probably suffered the least, being the least aware of what we were going through.

The passengers on the ship seemed different from those we had traveled with before, more determined to leave and with better means to start a new life. None of us knew that leaving China in 1949 would mean not seeing it again for another thirty years or more.

We finally arrived at Jilong, the port for Taibei, the capital of Taiwan. I still had my boys' clothes on. It was late in the evening, and Jilong, while not cold at this time of the year, was wet and uncomfortable. All of us were waiting by the curb for our transportation from the air force. I noticed two dock workers whispering to each other, pointing in our direction. My parents noticed it too but said nothing. Finally one of the men came over, somewhat timidly, and asked, "I beg your pardon, but my buddy and I have this bet going," pointing at me. "Is this a boy or girl?" My parents looked at each other and laughed. Fatigue of the journey forgotten, they laughed as if this were the best joke of the year. At last Mother said, rather loudly and proudly, "She is a girl, of course."

Part Two

BETWEEN EAST
AND WEST —
TAIWAN AND AMERICA

8

Roadside Flowers and My Truant Years

B ehind the Jingshui Elementary School was a wide area of farmland, with dirt roads winding down to more farmland. Some patches were uncultivated. Some had been turned into rice paddies and vegetable fields. Old-fashioned hut dwellings for farmers, with straw roofs and brick walls made of mud and dry hay, could be seen at a distance. Wild flowers stretched along the roads during spring, summer, and fall, but not during the unusually short winter of Taiwan. The flowers—red, yellow, orange, blue, purple, white—looked lonely but free against the sea of rice fields. Their pleasant smells mingled with the astringent odor of the grass and wet dirt of the rice fields, and stimulated the heart of a nine-year-old. I was out of school again, on a glorious day, to roam the countryside by myself.

When my family emigrated to Taiwan in 1949, I was six years old and was enrolled in the second grade in a school set up for the children of the Chinese Nationalist Air Force. Delighted to be with classmates who had gone through the

75

same experience of relocation from mainland China, I was enjoying myself in school, despite the new, unfamiliar curriculum and the government's requirement that only Mandarin Chinese be used in school.

A year later, Father was promoted to head an engineering unit in the remote town of Jingshui, a small farming community in central Taiwan. I was transferred to the only grammar school in town, Jingshui Elementary School, and assigned to the fourth grade, although I had only completed the first half of my third grade work. I managed to maintain my grades the first year, although I did find the school work difficult.

I tried to settle into the new environment. I even began to make friends in school with the farm children who came to school barefoot, carrying their only pair of shoes which they put on in the classroom.

Everything changed for me in the fifth grade, where the Japanese-trained teacher believed in and specialized in corporal punishment.

In this small village school, the effects of the fifty-year Japanese occupation of Taiwan could be felt everywhere. The teachers still preferred speaking Japanese to Chinese. Worse yet, when they castigated the students, they used rapid-fire Japanese, which completely baffled a newcomer like me. I needed to learn not only the Taiwanese dialect —which most of my classmates from the community spoke —but also choice words in Japanese.

The practice of corporal punishment in my Japanese-trained teacher's classroom was practically an art form. All the students were grouped according to their levels of achievement. What was so disturbing was that the higher the level, the heavier the punishment. The theory was that punishment is an honor bestowed only upon those chosen few capable of still further improving their performance. The poor students usually escaped such attention, as they were not worthy of the teacher's time.

The punishments were devised to inflict both psychological and physical pain. For psychological impact, a favorite method was for the teacher to write the less-than-perfect test score or the criticism of the student in unwashable red ink on the student's cheek, so that the rest of the world could join in the ridicule. The tools for physical punishment ranged from rulers, sticks, and brooms, to bare hands. Even the bare-hand method had its variations: boxing the ear, hitting the head with knuckles, pinching the cheek, pulling the hair, and bouncing the nose with the middle finger, and so on.

I watched in dismay as these punishments were handed out to others, and felt their pain when they came my way. By then I had mastered the new course materials and was considered one of the top students in class. Thus, if the teacher expected me to get a score of 98 and my actual score was 96, I received two strokes by one of the methods mentioned above, to remind me of the need to improve next time. I was even more distressed to find that most of my classmates seemed to completely accept these measures, particularly the good students. After each beating they would return to their seats, tears in their eyes from the pain but smiling proudly as if they had just received the supreme honor. I was horrified.

I had no one to turn to. For some reason, I never confided my troubles to my parents, probably assuming that they would not intervene. Nor was I totally convinced that parents in general were really against corporal punishment at school, since it was also practiced at home. I decided to take matters into my own hands—I stopped going to school whenever I could get away with it. I showed up at the proper time to take exams, turn in the assignments, and maintain good grades. I knew how important it was for me to meet my parents' expectations that I continued to do well in school.

Still interested in learning, I studied on my own and found the materials not too difficult to master without instruction. The practice of rigid teaching methods and learning by rote in the elementary school supported my truancy. As long as I had the class notes borrowed from my classmates, and the same math problems to solve, I could easily get good grades.

I started going round with a group of students not interested in learning. They made truancy a way of life. Together we were a little wild and even delinquent, roaming around the village to raid fruit trees in peoples' yards and to steal supplies from a stationery store in town. For reasons that never became clear, I was not caught and reported to my parents; they were under the impression that I dutifully attended school each day.

In the sixth grade, I had the same teacher. He offered tutoring classes after school for students interested in taking the entrance exam for middle school—free education in Taiwan in the 1950s was limited to the elementary level only. After graduation from elementary school many children went to work, especially farm children.

The teacher charged a tutoring fee for the extra effort on his part. Not wanting to appear different and convinced that I needed the tutoring, I signed up for his class. To my utter dismay the same punitive measures were carried into the tutoring class, more severely than before as the few teachers holding these special sessions competed with one another to see who could put more graduates into the middle school. Once again I stopped going to the class and finally told my father I had not found the tutoring very helpful. Father agreed and did not question me further. He wrote a rather formal note to the teacher asking for reimbursement of the tutoring fee.

I sensed that the note from Father must have touched some sensitive area, for the teacher's expression as he read the note I had brought him was complex. His face turned red, then white. Without saying a word, he went to his desk drawer to get the money for me. I wondered at the time whether he was angry. I was convinced that he might see the gesture as an insult to his teaching. And I had the audacity to ask for reimbursement!

Things went from bad to worse for me in school after this incident. Now determined to get even with me, the teacher maneuvered to get me elected class president. He probably knew how much I disliked the morning ritual led by the class president, that of gathering together the entire class and marching them to the athletic field for a pledge of allegiance and lecture by the school principal. A few years younger than most of my classmates, I was also one of the shortest. A few classmates, favorites of the teacher, would giggle incessantly as I gave the drill orders for the march. I would inevitably be criticized by the teacher for my inability to control the class. He laughed along with them at my ineptitude. It was torture to go to school every day. I knew what the teacher was trying to do, but I was not about to let it defeat me. It was a contest of wills, his and mine, and I had no doubt who was going to win, for I made up my mind then that no one in this world could ever get my spirits down. I practiced hard at the drill routines. I also became more assertive with my classmates when they got out of line during these morning exercises.

Finding friends was difficult for me in this elementary school. I knew I was different, part of a minority group from mainland China. The native Taiwanese students would shout at us, "Mainland pigs! Go home! We don't want you here!" The discrimination confused me, for it was a new experience to be considered an outsider by your countrymen. At home in the air force compound, life was a little easier. I made friends there, and over time became the ringleader of a small group. I had no qualms about picking a fight with anyone, boy or girl. In retrospect, I was probably taking out my frustrations regarding school through these fights. I was small but strong; even when my fights with the boys ended in cuts and bruises, I rarely cried.

Gradually I also made a few Taiwanese friends and found my reading ability an asset in winning friendship. Classmates began to approach me during recess imploring me to recite passages from a new book I had just read. I was willing to help others with their schoolwork, never feeling threatened by competition, much to the chagrin of the other good students in my class. I began to feel better about the school, despite the unrelenting vengeance of the teacher.

I tried to understand my teacher, convinced that he could not behave this way without good reasons. He was a plain-looking, frail man in his late twenties, with a stooped back and perpetual cough from chain-smoking. He seemed to be a loner, unlike the other male teachers of his age; he was single, and there was not even a hint of a romance in the air for him. He often spoke of the harsh treatment he had received under the Japanese regime and would tell us we could not imagine the cruelty he had suffered. Yet he also seemed genuinely devoted to the Japanese teaching method despite his loyalty to the new Republic and his delight that the Japanese occupation was finally over. The only female teacher he seemed close to, a big, jovial middle-aged woman, often teased him about his shyness around women. I observed how much this female teacher could push him around and how easily he blushed at the sight of any pretty woman. With the students, he was only comfortable when in total control of us.

I went through my sixth grade, half-frustrated, half-accepting the rules in school, always yearning for more freedom in life. I was the happiest when I roamed the countryside. I picked wild flowers from the roadside and put them in the diary I was beginning to keep as a remembrance of my lonely yet free moments. I learned to be alone and enjoy it. I was convinced life could be better and different. Feeling unsupported by the adults in my life, the teacher and my parents who were preoccupied with their own concerns at home and at work, I no longer saw adults as the absolute authority in my life.

Finally graduation day arrived. Students with good grade averages were given numerous awards during the graduation ceremony. Yet I received none. I understood this to be the work of my teacher, and tried to be philosophical. Some of my friends were indignant for they thought the teacher very unfair in his treatment of me. After the ceremony, which was difficult for me to sit through with these thoughts raging in my head, the teacher called the class together to give the final salutations. All of a sudden he announced to the class that he wanted to hand out a special present to a special student, and he proceeded to call me to the podium. I got up in disbelief, as he slowly took out of a briefcase two notebooks and handed them to me. I looked at them. They were badly scuffed and worn—throwaway objects, the poorest sort of gift he could bestow. In a flash I realized that this insult was his last attempt to break my spirit. Controlling my impulse to break down or throw the books, I took them from him with a deep bow and half of a smile. A friend came over to walk me home afterward. We walked on the dirt road beyond the school. In the open country air, without anyone looking but my friend, I cried for the first time since I had entered Jingshui Elementary School.

I knew I was intelligent and a good student. Lack of validation from this teacher did not alter my opinion about myself. I was nevertheless hurt and humiliated by his persistently unfair treatment, and from the burden I carried, within myself, at age nine and ten. I had to reach inside for all my reserves of strength and determination to survive those years.

With the entrance exam only a few months away and with no help from any special tutoring, I devised a study routine for myself. Father had by then been promoted to a higher position directing the air force's parachute manufacturing company, and we moved to a bigger house in town. The new house had a big, lovely garden with a mango tree and plum trees, and a ready-made swing. For three months I sat on this swing and studied each day until it was so dark that I could no longer read the fine print in my books.

I took the entrance exam along with thousands of other elementary school graduates from the region. To my and everyone else's surprise, I was the top winner on the list of fewer than one hundred accepted for the Jingshui Middle School. While I had never doubted my ability to pass the exam, I had not expected to do so well.

I became an instant celebrity. The news about this ten-year-old girl who had defeated all others for top place in the exams shook the small town. My parents took the news calmly. When congratulated by his friends, Father even joked that I had won the top prize because "when there is no tiger in the mountain, the monkey becomes king"—an old Chinese proverb that tended to diminish my victory. I was disappointed that he could not recognize the effort behind my achievement. But strangely, Father's praise, or lack of such, no longer meant much to me. I had become more self-reliant as a result of the horrible experience of dealing with the Japanese-trained teacher.

I was to have another unpleasant encounter with my teacher after that. My friends told me he was livid upon learning of my victory and was further embarrassed by his colleagues' inquiry as to whether I had taken his tutoring class. He tried a final blow, that of withholding my diploma. When I found out that he had not sent the diploma to me, after all of my classmates had received theirs, I went to see him. He said, rather indifferently, "Oh, yes, your diploma. Come back here tomorrow. You can have it." Not wanting to offend him, although I was no longer his student, I walked four miles home, ready to return the following day. I returned the next day to find him chatting with his colleagues in the teacher's lounge, completely ignoring me. I waited outside, standing, as there were no seats available. Then he got up and left the room. I was getting anxious that he might not return when one teacher who knew me by sight came out to ask me whether he could be of any assistance. I told him the situation. He was furious. "That bastard! He's gone for the day. Look, let me see what I can do." He proceeded to go to my teacher's desk to pry open the drawer. At the bottom of the drawer was my diploma, the only one left in the drawer. He handed it to me over my profuse thanks. I was worried that he might get into trouble. He said, "Don't you worry about a thing. I can take care of myself."

I left the elementary school for the last time, determined never to return again. I walked the four miles home along the familiar dirt roads. The wild flowers were soothing to my frayed emotions. A number of times I was tempted to throw my diploma into the river. But I didn't.

Luckily my experience in middle school proved stimulating and rewarding. I found no corporal punishment there.

One day, as I was walking home after a seventh grade class, I passed by the street leading to the elementary school. I saw my old teacher walking toward me. Time had put enough distance between us, but I still dreaded the sight of him. Yet I did something I was to be proud of for a long time—I did not avoid him. When he came closer I looked at him, took a deep bow and greeted him, "Good afternoon, teacher." He appeared shocked and embarrassed and he was tongue-tied for a few seconds. Then he said, almost cordially, "Good afternoon, Murong."

9

In Memory of Teacher Liu

When my teacher, Mr. Liu from Jingshui Middle school, died at last after a prolonged battle with liver cancer, I was already in graduate studies at the University of Michigan. I learned of his early death from my parents, who on my behalf had sent the appropriate paper-flower wreaths and white linen to his funeral in Jingshui, Taiwan.

Having just read the letter from my parents about Mr. Liu's death, I walked out of Mosher Hall, the women's residence on campus, and saw coeds sunbathing on the lush, green lawn. Saddened by the news and dazed by the afternoon sun, I was struck by the contrasting mood of my happy "kids," as I called them (for at twenty-one I was the resident advisor at Mosher Hall in charge of the freshmen and sophomore women). My own youth flashed back. I thought about Mr. Liu, who had died thousands of miles away, and about his unfulfilled dreams. I thought about the many years I had had him as my teacher and how I would now not have the chance to recompense him with some of the fruit of his labor.

Mr. Liu's last letter to me, written a few weeks before his death, still showed his fighting spirit:

> When your letter arrived the other day with the enclosed money for my treatment (no doubt from your meager scholarship), I was moved to tears. That I had had a few shots of morphine to kill the pain on that day no longer mattered. I know you are concerned about my condition; rest assured that I will fight back, just as I have always fought back. This time I may even surprise myself.

He lost his battle with the illness. His many years of near-impoverishment as a middle school teacher had left him weak and exhausted. He died in his late forties, leaving his wife and five children. He also left behind the memories of his students, for Mr. Liu had been teacher to many students. He had been one of my favorite teachers at Jingshui Middle School.

In the 1950s student life in Taiwan was dampened by the political climate under the Chiang Kai-shek regime. The conservative and restrictive martial law was in full force, with a military presence in all segments of society. Each middle school was assigned a coordinator of military education to promote the political ideology of the Nationalist government and to teach basic military skills to the students. The position of the military coordinator was usually held by a veteran officer whose sole experience was on the battlefield, his sole preoccupation, obedience and discipline. Assigned as the eyes and ears of the government in the school, these military coordinators also served another purpose: surveillance of civilian activities. Freedom of speech was limited and open criticism of the government prohibited.

I remember one teacher of geography, a young graduate from a leading university in Taiwan. He had been unusually candid in his criticism of martial law under the ruling party, and the limited freedom of the academic community which he felt should have been exempt from the restrictions imposed on the rest of society. One day he mysteriously disappeared from the school. I later found out that he had been sent to a remote island off the coast of Taiwan to be "re-educated" after one of his colleagues had reported his open criticism to the coordinator of military education. He returned, two years later, a broken man, subdued and depressed. When asked, he would not comment on his experience. We understood that he did not want ever again to pay such a price for earnest criticism of government policies.

We students accepted the need to follow the government ideology along with its necessary ritual. We bowed to the portraits of Sun Yat-sen, the founding father of the Chinese republic, and of Chiang Kai-shek, the president of the Nationalist government; we saluted each time we mentioned their names in a public address. We learned to leave one extra space between their names and surrounding words in our writing, to show our utmost reverence for them.

Military education was provided to both the male and female students. Military marching and close-drill formations as well as the use of firearms were part of the training curriculum. I was unable to develop any skills in the latter. Try as I might, pulling the trigger of a rifle at an imagined enemy was too much for me. Like most of my classmates,

I managed to tolerate the weekly training, for accepting it was easier and less painful than refusing.

The use of firearms in military training was always problematic, for blanks and real bullets were used interchangeably. We had a tragic accident at Jingshui Middle School when one student, for fun during the recess, shot at another student—and the bullets turned out to be real. The day of the accident, I was cutting the lawn with my classmates on the athletic field—we used hand lawn-knives—as part of the mandatory physical labor. We heard a shot from the rooftop of the firearms storage room, then a scream, "He's been shot! He's been shot! Get him to a doctor!" Moments later we saw a male student, with blood all over his body, being carried on the back of another student, with the military coordinator trailing behind. A few hours later the unfortunate youth died in the hospital. The youth who had accidentally shot him was arrested and was sentenced to six years in prison. No charges were ever brought against the school personnel for negligence in monitoring the use of firearms. But civil rights were a foreign concept in Taiwan.

Most of the time the students accepted the rules set down by the school authorities and the government. During national holidays we were allowed to skip class to parade down the streets shouting, "Long live President Chiang" or "Down with the running dogs of the Communist bandits," demonstrating our support of the anti-Communist campaign. The local citizens had become used to our processions and made room for us, smiling indulgently at these crazy students. As class representative I led my class on numerous occasions in the parades, we shouted at the top of our lungs, enjoying ourselves even more because of the day off from classes.

Those were impressionable years. What may appear to have been oppressive practices by the authorities were taken for granted by the students. And no wonder: having no alternative, adults and children alike accepted what the political and social systems handed down to them.

The learning environment in the middle school was fair to good. Left with few opportunities to step out of line, most students were hardworking and attentive and respectful toward their teacher. This was reinforced by the long Chinese Confucian tradition: Honor thy teacher. The teachers, no matter how inadequate, received the utmost respect from their students who not only obeyed their orders in school, but also performed services such as running errands for the teachers' families after school.

In the middle school, ancient Chinese, a difficult language to master, was taught side by side with modern Chinese, which is more colloquial and closer to everyday usage. Old gentlemen in their long mandarin robes were often chosen to teach Chinese. They brought to class not only their preference for the ancient form of the language but also their traditional teaching methods—teaching line by line from the book, followed by memorization and recitation. Student questions in class were not encouraged, justified by a quote from an ancient poet: "Learning is to be enjoyed, not to be fully understood." Not that there were no exciting teachers; there were quite a few math and science teachers who could turn algebra, geometry, biology, and chemistry into fascinating worlds for us. And one prolific art teacher, trained at the Shanghai Academy of Arts, was particularly good at stimulating our individual creativity. But many teachers held the culturally prevalent values about female students—that women never would amount to anything important in life. One chemistry teacher was known to proclaim that even the only thing women were good at—cooking—did not bring them any recognition because the most famous chefs are male. When I asked him whether that was because women had not been given the opportunity for employment as chefs, he brushed aside the question by arguing that men always outperform women in every walk of life. To make matters worse for the female students, the greatest teacher in Chinese history, Confucius, held a low opinion of women. A well-known quotation from Confucius—"Two kinds of people are difficult company, the narrow-minded and women"—was used time and again by male teachers whenever they became frustrated with the more assertive female students. Such bias in school was supported by the home environment. Most families did not encourage their daughters to pursue an education. Some families were already making arrangements for their daughters' weddings upon graduation from middle school. Arranged marriages were still an accepted practice among the native Taiwanese.

To preserve the hierarchical difference between teachers and students, a social distance was maintained. Students knew their rightful place in the prescribed power structure: students were at the bottom.

It was therefore more than a pleasant surprise the day Mr. Liu walked into Chinese literature class and announced that he wanted to be a friend to his students. He was a short, plump, bespectacled man in a three-piece suit, smiling at us, unlike the more severe demeanor maintained by other teachers to show their superior position. He went on to let us know that he preferred *baihua*, the modern Chinese, to ancient Chinese, not only because the former was more practical, but also because the value system of ancient

China had kept China a backward country for centuries. He then pointed out some of the many flaws in Confucius' teaching, not the least of which was the less significant position of women in society. We, the female students, were ready to jump out of our seats to cheer. Here, finally, was a man, a teacher to boot, to whom we could relate.

We soon learned that Mr. Liu had been carrying on a national debate in the press over the written language and whether we should use the original or the simplified characters. Mr. Liu supported using the simplified characters. His reasoning: the time saved in writing the simplified form of the Chinese characters could be devoted to the modernization of China. He was to meet with strong opposition from the traditionalists and the government. The Nationalist government had a tendency to oppose anything supported by Communist China as a matter of policy, and simplified Chinese had been pushed by the Communists in the 1950s as a major national initiative.

Active and outspoken in class, Mr. Liu appeared to be a different person in private. He gave the impression of a man deep in thought, walking with his head down, eyes concentrating on the ground. He did not seem to have any close friends and spent much time by himself. He was rather scornful of the idleness of his colleagues. "Knowing that our lives are so brief and precious, why don't they try to improve their learning?" His intense concern with learning was obviously not shared by many others.

Mr. Liu was a demanding teacher. He challenged the students to be creative and inquisitive, a new experience for us. He changed dramatically the usual format of composition—a two-hour impromptu writing exercise—by not giving any suggestions for a topic for the composition. A typical class with him would find us scribbling down an outline of a subject, conceived entirely on our own, before using Chinese brush and ink to put down the final draft on rice paper. He would pick up a few sample writings and read them aloud in class. Mine was often used as an example of good writing.

During my first year in high school, Father had been promoted to commander of the air base and my family moved to the house previously occupied by the mayor of the town during the Japanese occupation. Closer now to the middle school and to the teachers' residences, located at the foot of the hill behind the middle school, I became a regular visitor at my teachers' houses. Students dropping in was considered normal and welcome. My favorite stop was Mr. Liu's house.

At the young age of 29, Mr. Liu had so excelled in his career as a middle school teacher that he had been selected as the principal of a middle school in northern China. His career was abruptly terminated when the Communists took over the school, forcing Mr. Liu to leave his hometown and his extended family behind. He left China with his wife and young children, and after an initial struggle to regain his teaching credentials in the Taiwan system, he was able to obtain a full-time teaching post with Jingshui Middle School. Mr. Liu, like many teachers I had met at the middle school, belonged to the influx of qualified teaching personnel from the mainland who were trying, with difficulty, to regain their places in the educational system. Disillusionment and disenchantment were common among them. Longing for the good old days that would never return, they were less enthusiastic about the present and the future. Here lay the difference between Mr. Liu and his teaching colleagues from mainland China. Mr. Liu would not give up enriching his learning, and expanding his horizons. When I met him he was a prolific writer and a regular contributor to newspapers and literary magazines. He was busy working on a book on modern Chinese literature.

Mr. Liu was a "feminist" teacher before the term had any meaning in Taiwan. He practiced what he believed —women could accomplish anything they set out to do— not only in school but also at home. He had no sons, but he had high expectations for his daughters. Mr. Liu was the only adult male in his generation from whom I never once heard regret at not having any male children. He also had a high regard for his wife, who had been a teacher in the middle school where he was the principal. He fondly called her "my woman"; we thought the greeting irreverent as it implied a crude, blatantly disrespectful connotation in Chinese, but he had simply translated the Western meaning into Chinese directly.

I sought advice on my readings. My sustained contact with him was a key to my own development as an inquisitive student. The special readings suggested by Mr. Liu all had a common theme: that which was traditional was undesirable; Western ideas were superior to those of the Chinese. While I fully embraced his teaching about the equal place women should hold in the society, I was less willing to forsake the entire Chinese heritage. We would have lively discussions about the good and bad of our cultural "baggage," the restrictive political and social climate in Taiwan, and the potential for inspiring a vibrant, outreaching people. Yet I believed that one could be critical and analytical without losing compassion for, and acceptance of, the differences in others. This was more difficult for him to accept, as he continued to hold contempt for believers in the traditional values of Confucianism. But the fact that he allowed my different views to be heard was a new experience for me. Students were rarely offered the opportunity to differ from their teachers.

Mr. Liu was the only adult male in whom I had confided my troubled adolescent romance with a boy I had met in high school and which continued even after I left to go to college. Mr. Liu's discretion about my personal affairs was always reassuring to me, and he never once betrayed my confidence to my parents. It was also unusual, given the unspoken agreement between the school and the family that any outside contact between male and female students was to be reported and stopped. In fact, the principal of the school, a friend of my father's, had more than once confiscated love letters addressed to me and turned them over to my parents. Never critical or judgmental, Mr. Liu understood my need to go over my feelings with a sympathetic adult. "You have to find your own answers in life about these relationships," he would say. "But you must first find out what you want from life."

As close as his house was to mine, Mr. Liu never had any real contact with my parents except on one unusual occasion—the annual typhoon season—when all the low-lying houses in the immediate area were flooded and we had to abandon them at a moment's notice. All the families went up to the middle school for shelter as it was on higher ground. Mr. Liu greeted my parents for the first time in a crowded room with hungry and restless children running around and adults looking harassed. These were not pleasant surroundings for an introduction, yet I thought all of them gave one another a cool though polite reception. For some reason my parents had not expressed an interest in getting to know Mr. Liu, even though they knew of my special relationship with him.

Mr. Liu seemed to have a special perception of my lonely position. Already somewhat distant from my own family, I was becoming disenchanted with what the middle school had to offer although I maintained my honor roll standing until I graduated. In my high school yearbook, his inscription reads:

> The better the quality of the music, the fewer will appreciate it; it is not the fault of the musician, but the lack of understanding of the audience.

This was written during the time I had become more aware of my own search for a higher plane in life—I had outgrown what Jingshui Middle School had to offer. While I had made a few friends, I was becoming more aware of the different goals I had in life. Mr. Liu saw and understood my struggle.

After I left Jingshui Middle School and found more young women like myself at college there would be many occasions on which I would reflect on Mr. Liu's inscription and the special effort he had made to lend a helping hand to a young woman trying to come to terms with herself. There would be other teachers like him with whom I would come in contact after I left Jingshui. But Mr. Liu will always have a special place in my heart.

CHAPTER
10

College Life
and Expectations

On the outskirts of Taizhong, atop Dadu mountain in central Taiwan, is Donghai University, a small Christian college where I spent four years learning more about the world outside. But I began with the world of Donghai itself. On a clear night one could see not only the stars, which seemed close enough to be touched, but also the city lights below in the Taizhong valley. Viewed from the top of the hill, this scene inevitably gave one the feeling of being in another world: Donghai was and remained that mythical place where dreams were made and, when inevitably broken, were replaced with new ones.

My parents had always assumed that I would go to college. Thanks to their assumption, entering college was something I had taken for granted, unlike my classmates from Jingshui Middle School. The majority of them would not seek a college education for reasons quite unrelated to their individual capabilities. Even though it was then acceptable for young women to obtain a college education

—after all, China had made public education available to women four decades earlier—sending a daughter to college was still a major decision, difficult for most families. Besides, some parents raised the question of what purpose it served for a woman to finish college only to get married and have children. Perhaps the college experience would make it possible to find a better husband, some parents reasoned. Others assumed that a college education might help the young woman to be more independent in life. My parents held the latter position.

I first saw Donghai during my senior year in high school. I had learned about its barren mountain setting, its emphasis on both liberal arts and science, and its small size of eight hundred students. More important, its first graduating class was in 1959, the year I entered. I made a special visit and was immediately attracted to its surroundings of dark red earth and open fields, and its subtle Chinese architecture with strong modern influences, designed by I.M. Pei. I felt a sense of belonging—I wanted to be part of this special world.

The island-wide college entrance exam was a grueling three-day event. The selection of a college depended entirely on the test scores in six subjects; all middle school academic records were left out of the consideration. Luckily I did well enough to be awarded a scholarship, with Donghai as my first choice. At sixteen, I left home for the first time, armed with nothing but enthusiasm for a new learning environment.

Arriving at Donghai were young men and women from all parts of Taiwan and Southeast Asia. Some came to Donghai as their first choice, others more reluctantly, preferring larger campuses. But no one could be indifferent to their college experience. Up on Dadu mountain, suspended in time and space, there was no escape but to face one another and to face oneself. Out of their individual homes, the entering class now became part of the Donghai family.

Several aspects of Donghai promoted this shared feeling. The availability of faculty members, who also lived on campus within walking distance from the student dormitories, facilitated after-class communication and learning. The work-study program enabled students with financial needs to maintain a minimum standard of living. The requirement that all students participate in unpaid dormitory housekeeping duties reduced class differences among the students.

I quickly got to know most of my college classmates, given the small class size. Over time, eight of us, all close friends, became known as the women with aspirations for promoting a higher standard of expectations for all women on campus.

I first met Cong, one of our eight, at a freshmen party. She had been asked to sing that night—someone must have heard about her singing talent—and she was an instant hit. Her soprano voice, delicate but rich in timbre, mesmerized the group. She was as bright as she was talented, having graduated with top honors from a middle school near Taibei. Finding ourselves going to the same classes our first year, we became good friends. Before the first year was out we had pulled together a small group of eight women and made plans to share rooms adjacent to one another the following year. The eight of us would continue to be neighbors until we graduated.

Our area became known in the residence hall as "Westgate Square," the busiest street in the capital. After supper, women from the rest of the residence hall would come in and out of our rooms because we had the most fun and laughter. On evenings when we did not rush to the library—all of us were conscientious students in different majors—we would often hold an impromptu dance party and try out new steps, or stroll down the road with a banjo in hand and sing the songs we had just learned.

Of the eight, Cong was the romantic and the dreamer. She was infatuated with the poet in our class, a talented student who had won acclaim in Taiwan for his prose and poetry before entering college. Their up-and-down romance, stretching over four years of college, would lead to an unhappy marriage and a divorce ten years later. But at Donghai, with her love new and unsettling, she would read his poetry, a volume hand-bound in blue cloth, which he had given her as a present. Sitting across the big desk we shared as roommates, I would be moved to tears by the beauty of the poetry. The night breeze came in through the screen door leading to our patio. We would then go out on the patio to watch the city lights in the valley below. I was there whenever Cong returned from her usual fight with her poet, swearing she would not see him anymore. But I knew she would be out the door in no time when he called her again. And Cong was there the day I burned old love letters from my first romance with a middle-school boy named Chen. Together we watched the smoke go up against the gray rainy sky, as gloomy as my mood.

There were close to two hundred Donghai women on campus, out of eight hundred students. The Donghai women showed their special brand of arrogance each time they walked down the college mall, passing by the Arts and Science buildings, the library, and the Administration Building, with books in their arms and their noses in the air—leaving the love-struck Donghai men completely helpless. To get a girl to go out took persuasion and perseverance and the patience of a saint. It was as if the Donghai women consciously or unconsciously had set out to turn the tables for thousands of less privileged women, to show the men that women were a force to be reckoned with.

Interaction between the sexes followed well-prescribed rules. The girls waited for the boys to call. Once she accepted the invitation of a Donghai man, a woman became committed to going out with him for the remainder of her college stay, unless some particular dramatic event interfered with the courtship. This pattern of dating reinforced the togetherness of the "pairs". Once a woman was paired off no other potentially interested man would dare ask her for a date or vie for her attention.

Our group did not care for this rigid and constricting pattern of dating and most of us remained "uncommitted" until the last year in college. Our acceptance of dates with different men raised eyebrows, but we were determined to break new ground for the interaction between men and women at Donghai. We wanted to demonstrate that men and women could and should be friends before any other relationship was formed. To prove this point, we set out to befriend a group of young men of similar mind and inclination, and together we formed a support group for conversation and learning, but not romance.

We found that men had much to offer with their unique perspective on life. They were less burdened by family constraints (boys growing up in China always had more freedom than girls), and less concerned about the opinions of others, concentrating on what was right and rational. They were more action-oriented; problems were to be resolved by "doing something about it," and they were wonderful companions to help us out of our blues. Once Cong was upset about a professor's pointing out a logical flaw in one of her term papers. Our male friends comforted her by putting on a surprise rabbit roast and outing next to the Buddhist temple. Cong quickly forgot her misery as we laughed about the monks' role in our feast—they had captured and cooked the rabbit for us despite their rigid vegetarian diet and religious principles of "no killing."

Perhaps this remained one of the most valuable lessons I learned at Donghai—that men and women can relate to one another on an equal basis, with candor and support, without the tensions of romantic relationships. Even long after some of us had formed romantic relationships, we still faithfully kept our male friends, and our gatherings continued on as before.

Not that we were without conflict or tension on a different level. A couple of the men and women in our group drifted into the more usual male-female relationship. Some wanted to, but did not succeed in changing the nature of their pure friendship. Most of us women kept the men as friends, not only to prove a point, but because we had come to value what male friendship could offer.

Donghai had its share of troubled romances and tragic affairs. During my four years, there was one suicide, by a male student following a failed love affair; a suicide attempt by a female student, from rejection by a male student; and several nervous breakdowns. Some students went on to further romantic difficulties after graduation. In a way, Donghai reflected the changing culture of Taiwan. Courtships between men and women existed side by side with marriages arranged by parents.

There were, however, definite rules of conduct at Donghai, as elsewhere in Taiwan. Marriages among college students were most unusual and very much frowned upon. There was only one in the four years I was at Donghai.

The Donghai women did not even smoke. Coming back to the women's residence after curfew hours after being out dancing was probably the worst infringement of the rules.

Nurtured and protected in this close environment, the students devoted most of their energy to studying. In the classroom, the gender roles blurred. The best excelled and there were no obstacles put in the way of women's achievements. For the first time, the young women were freed from preconceived notions about the limits of their ability to learn. In such an institution of higher learning, the sky was the limit.

Contributing to this enlightened environment was the presence of young English and American teachers, men and women interested in sharing more than just their language. The Oberlin "reps," as we called the graduates from Oberlin College selected to teach English classes at Donghai, brought more than their knowledge and vitality. They came with a more relaxed attitude about the interaction between students and teachers. This meeting of East and West was quickly welcomed. Cultural norms can be learned, and the students soon learned to address their young English and American teachers with less formality than their Chinese professors. From the standpoint of these young teachers, adjusting to a different culture was not overly difficult. Their initial awkwardness was easily alleviated by the open Chinese hospitality on campus. They communicated well with the students, but their encounter with the Chinese professors often proved to be more difficult. For years there was a schism between the two faculty groups, each holding its position regarding the institutional direction, and each claiming a sizable following.

The Western influence on campus came from other parts of the island as well. Most of the popular movies were

Western and the youth tuned in to rock and roll. In addition, the constant presence of American military personnel continued all through the 1950s and 1960s.

As a Christian college, Donghai offered optional religious studies and services. The chapel was built the year I graduated. While the number of students converted to Christianity was limited, the common values of mutual aid and self-help were deeply held at Donghai. The campus always came to life during the Christmas celebrations. Less obtrusive were the routine Bible classes, attended by believers and nonbelievers alike.

The political climate in Taiwan had an impact on campus life, perhaps less noticeable in college than in the middle school. There was some apathy toward politics and more open discussion of government policies, all in the name of objective research and learning. In my junior year the first National Youth Congress was held on Yangming Mountain, sponsored by the ruling Guomindang party. I was the delegate from Donghai. Along with delegates from various colleges and universities, we were struck by the high volume of propaganda materials we had to go through at the convention—the Congress had been promoted as a new initiative to develop an agenda for Chinese youth. As it turned out, with the continuing lecturing on anti-Communism and guest speeches by refugees from mainland China, the agenda for youth was totally overshadowed by the government's anti-Communism campaign. I was not alone in feeling like a pawn.

On the last day of the conference, President Chiang Kai-shek came to greet us. We had been asked to vacate the auditorium so that the security personnel could check for any concealed assassination weapons. Chiang was not a bad speaker, and after his brief speech he passed down the line of students, smiling and nodding: "Very good," was his favorite greeting in public. He was then whisked away by his security guards. I was nevertheless disenchanted with the party line and the lack of true inspirational leadership.

But our life at Donghai was largely insulated from political and even religious influences, and Donghai students wasted no time in finding fun. Students discovered two legendary hiking attractions: Dream Valley and the Old Castle. Dream Valley, a dry riverbed beyond the women's residence covered with huge rocks, became, over time, the site of camp fires, parties, and rendezvous. The Old Castle, in fact leftover bunkers from the Japanese occupation, provided an ideal place for picnics and ventures inside the bunkers themselves. Complementing these outdoor activities were sports, square dances, and popular Western dances. It was not unusual to find each evening filled with scheduled and unscheduled events on and off campus.

There were the usual clubs and societies to join. I took on as many as my schedule would allow. My favorite one remained the Donghai Drama Club, of which I was the president for two years. Totally immersed in the twice-yearly production of plays, with their late rehearsals and hectic performance schedules, I thoroughly enjoyed the responsibilities of a president: selecting plays, putting together a cast, setting budgets, choosing an artistic director, and building sets. When I could not find a willing performer, I doubled as actress. My friends from the group of eight were frequent volunteers for these productions. Some of them were cast in our plays.

The final year found us more subdued and reflective. With the graduation closing in on us, the future loomed ahead. How would we venture forth from Donghai, this protected environment? We knew we would have to, for that was what Donghai had prepared us for during these years. We knew the outside world would be very different and, for women especially, the reality of our limited role in Taiwanese society would dampen our enthusiasm for any pursuit we might attempt. Many of us decided on graduate studies, rationalizing that to make it in the real world, women had to be better prepared than men.

Of the eight, seven of us decided on graduate studies and one decided to return to Singapore for matrimony. May, whose boyfriend had gone to the United States the year before, was determined to follow him there. Guo, who had changed boyfriends as frequently as she had changed her classes, was also interested in educational opportunities abroad. Ting, the most innocent of all as she had never once dated during her four years at Donghai, had a science career in mind. Lee, a girl from a rich Taiwanese family, was going to show her conservative family that women can excel. She would be the first daughter to venture abroad by enrolling in a graduate program in the United States. June, whose sister had gone to the United States to study physics, also had additional education in mind. Seven of us would be scattered all over the United States, in different programs. I had applied for and received a special scholarship, the Levi Barbour Scholarship, from the University of Michigan, where I would be studying social work, a subject still largely unexplored in Taiwan. My parents had no objection to my personal plans despite their apprehension that I might not be able to make the transition from the protected environment to which I had become accustomed.

Only recently have women had access to higher education in China. Educational opportunity for women was mentioned in the constitution of the new Chinese Republic founded in 1911, and the 1923 Chinese Civil Code theoretically gave women equal access to education. But before Liberation, social attitudes and economic realities severely limited a woman's chance for obtaining even elementary schooling.

My paternal and maternal grandmothers never went to school at all. For my mother's generation a high school education was considered highly unusual for a girl, and a university education was available only to the rich and powerful, and even then, only for the daughters of a few enlightened families. An educated Chinese woman could choose from only a very few career paths: teaching, nursing, or raising a family—as was true for her Western counterpart at that time.

The prescribed virtues for Chinese women were similar to those of Victorian Western women, with one exception. While the female virtues of obedience, patience, and self-denial were imposed on Chinese and Western women alike, in China a respectable woman was expected to also be illiterate. A well-known Chinese proverb argues bluntly, "A virtuous woman is an ignorant woman." A woman's calling in life was to learn the domestic skills and to serve men.

This attitude survived well into the 20th century. Han Suyin's poignant account in *Birdless Summer* of her marriage to her Chinese husband in the 1940s offers the clearest personal account of the attitude of an educated Chinese man of that period. In one of the early dialogues with her husband Pao, before their divorce, he told Han Suyin that she must "learn the Ancient virtues, and one of them is obedience. 'A woman of talent is not a virtuous woman.'"[1] Even with somewhat improved access to education under the Republic, the education of a Chinese woman was not for her own learning, but for the "support of the husband and the teaching of her children."

I grew up in a household where learning was encouraged. Though limited in their educational backgrounds, both Grandmother Li and my first aunt were avid readers. Thus finding a corner in the house to read was considered a more desirable activity for me than roaming the streets. Living close to the elementary school also encouraged my early entry into the school system. By age four, I was completing the first grade with male and female classmates a few years older, which seemed to be accepted by my family.

Mother's own lack of interest in domestic activities also steered me away from learning all the skills a young girl was supposed to acquire. I did not learn how to cook, sew, knit, or do needlework until I was well into my adulthood, when I taught myself these skills.

I was allowed to explore my own interest in learning, which remained strong even under adverse circumstances —the repeated family moves, the tyrannical Japanese-trained teacher in elementary school in Jingshui, and the unimaginative teaching in my middle school.

In Taiwan, the attitude toward women going on to college had improved by the 1960s. It was no longer taboo for women to excel in school. But finding suitable employment was quite another matter. The work place still discriminated against women—the better jobs usually went to men. I left the island not long after graduating from college, after working in the Municipal Health Department for a year. I had discovered that there was no future for career advancement there.

When I first met American college students at the University of Michigan, I was dismayed to find the same conflict in the United States: achieving in school and losing in the workplace. Although there was a higher proportion of female college students in America, and far more employment opportunities for women graduates, they did not get as good jobs as men. And women were still torn by the seemingly irreconcilable conflict between career and family. When I returned to school to work on my doctorate in the 1970s, although women were freer in their personal lives, the choice of career or family was still a troubling dilemma.

By the 1980s, both in China and the United States, the number of college educated women entering the work force had increased dramatically. But their upward mobility is still restricted. In China, and in other parts of Asia, few women are yet able to advance beyond middle level executive positions in the male dominated power structure.

11

Ann Arbor

A nn Arbor looked very small from the air. Rows and rows of tiny toy-like houses were lined up across a small strip of land. Then I saw the Detroit Metropolitan Airport where I would be landing, after flying for two days directly from Taibei. Saying good-bye to my family had not been as difficult as I had thought it would be. On the way over I had enjoyed the night view of Tokyo where we had a brief stop at the airport, then Waikiki Beach in Honolulu for an afternoon. I saw my fiance off at the Chicago airport before changing flights for Ann Arbor, my final destination.

Not knowing a soul in Ann Arbor, I had not notified anyone of my arrival. I got off the plane and asked for the best way to get to the school. I got into a waiting airport limousine with my suitcase, weighed down by the books I thought I would need. After what seemed to be an endless drive—I was finding it increasingly difficult to keep my eyes open—the limousine finally arrived at the University of Michigan Student Union, its last stop.

I got out and paid the fare plus a tip by watching how others did it. Tipping was new for me. I looked for a phone to call my temporary roommate, arranged for by the school, while I located an apartment in town. Unfortunately my roommate-to-be was out. A visitor answered the phone who knew about my pending arrival. Just as I wondered about how to get there with my large suitcase, two young men walked toward me with friendly smiles and asked if I needed any help. They turned out to be two Danish students waiting for an evening activity at the Union. I gave them the address and they promptly guided me through the door to their beat-up Chevy. At the front door of my new residence, they waved a quick good-bye with a resounding wish of good luck.

Thus began by first exposure to this friendly town. I would meet many more helpful people during my two year stay on campus, their kindness not always properly reciprocated.

I was soon apartment hunting. With addresses in hand, I would walk up and down the streets checking out the locations and distance to the main campus where I would be attending most of my classes. One rooming house close to the campus seemed a good possibility for me, but later I changed my mind because it lacked cooking facilities. The landlady, a plump woman in her fifties, was anxious for me to rent it, but more interested in my meeting my fellow countrymen. "I want you to meet this very nice young man from Hong Kong." Ignoring my protest she drove me over to another apartment and introduced me to a Chinese graduate student who turned out to be an acquaintance of my temporary roommate. I laughed at the attempt at match-making even in the States.

Many foreign students came to Ann Arbor in the 1960s. I met students from all over Asia, including Taiwan, Hong Kong, Singapore, Korea, and Japan. The Chinese students changed my previous picture of overseas Chinese intellectuals. As a group, with only a few exceptions, they tended to be petty, self-centered, myopic in their outlook on life, and resistant to learning about the society around them. They tended to socialize as a group. Academically they performed well; culturally they remained alienated. Cynicism seemed to permeate this group. They were cynical about the Chiang Kai-shek regime in Taiwan, skeptical about Mao Zedong's policies in China, disenchanted with Western culture.

I was getting a large dose of new information about mainland China. The anti-Communist propaganda in Taiwan was seriously challenged here. More confusing for me was the emerging Taiwanese Independence Movement, which had been forcefully silenced in Taiwan by the Nationalist government. I heard the movement leader Chen Yide, who came to the campus to discuss the Taiwanese reaction to the May 28 incident of 1947, the bloody massacre of native Taiwanese by the local Guomindang regime. For the first time, I began to realize that this was an angry repressed group, subjugated and ruled by the mainlander minority, of which I was one. A sobering lesson for the daughter of an Air Force general of the Chiang Kai-shek regime.

But even more eye-opening experiences awaited me at the University. For the Civil Rights movement 1964 was the watershed year. A number of my classmates from the School of Social Work had marched in Selma, Alabama with Martin Luther King, Jr. and had been jailed. We were busy signing petitions to get them out of jail, as well as writing petitions to President Johnson to stop the Vietnam War. Along with my classmates, I joined the "teach-ins", out of curiosity at first, but was soon convinced it was also my cause to oppose this war. I was surprised to discover how close the philosophy and values taught at the School of Social Work were to my own.

A classmate took me to demonstrate against a speech given by George Rockwell of the American Nazi Party. We formed a silent and peaceful picket line in front of the lecture hall where he was speaking that evening. I was stimulated and challenged to think beyond my immediate concerns. Not that I did not have immediate personal concerns. I depended on my scholarship to pay tuition and expenses, and I needed to do well enough to keep the stipend. I arrived for my first year at school with less than two hundred dollars, saved from one year's employment in Taiwan. I did not want to ask my parents for money. It was a sink or swim period for me.

The first week in graduate school showed me that the transition from my education in the Far East to an American graduate school was not going to be easy. I drew a blank in my first social policy class, not even understanding the course assignments. Language was still a barrier for me, particularly speaking and writing. The open structure of the graduate school program also meant that I would have to do more independent study on my own.

I was worried, but not ready to give up. Counting on my own ability to pull through any situation, I studied harder, and soon became comfortable with the course materials. I discovered that I had an ability to grasp subtle nuances, and my commitment to the helping profession grew steadily as time went on. By the end of the first semester, I had made good enough grades to keep the scholarship.

But my studies would be arduous throughout my two years in Ann Arbor. As I became more proficient in the language and the subjects, I felt even more acutely my deficiencies and the need to learn more.

I had signed up to be assigned to an American host family who would act as a support to me and provide a link to American family life. I was chosen by Mary and Jerry, a young couple with two small children. Jerry was a pathology resident at the University Hospital and Mary was a nurse by training. I was invited to all family gatherings and holiday celebrations. Both Mary and Jerry exemplified the best of a Christian, middle-class family—they were kind, helpful, and believed in family integrity. I got to know their two children well and enjoyed reading bedtime stories to their five-year-old Cathy. I took a particular liking to their son Billy who was barely two years old and had a rare sensitivity for a child his age. One evening after supper Billy took me to their dining room window and exclaimed, "Look, Alice, an evening star!" He was a human being after my own heart.

I gradually built a support group around me. For studies I had a few close classmates with whom to exchange views. I was surprised and flattered when my American classmates asked to borrow my lecture notes. For social support I joined in the general activities on campus, in addition to the various cultural activities of the Chinese student body. One Chinese woman, a graduate of Smith college, became my close friend. I visited her often and even confided in her about my troubled relationship with my fiance.

That first winter in Ann Arbor I saw snow for the first time since I had left mainland China in 1949. The first day of snow I rushed out of my apartment to feel its soft fall. But snow also brought hardship for travelers. On our way to Detroit for our weekly field work, my classmate, Grace, and I were stranded in the biggest snow storm ever to hit Michigan. Abandoning the car, Grace and I were lucky to find a taxi back to the campus.

At the end of the first year I decided to move out of the apartment and into a dormitory so that I might mingle more with American students. The idea of becoming a resident advisor appealed to me so I applied for the post. During the job interview I was asked, "You have been here in this country for less than a year. What makes you think you are qualified for the job?" I replied, "While I am from a different culture, the main concerns college students face are universal: boy friends and homesickness. I understand both problems well." I got the job.

Beneath my confident exterior I was nervous about my new responsibility for the forty coeds at Mosher Hall. I found the freshmen and sophomores easy to relate to, but not necessarily the residence administration. University residence halls seem to attract frustrated matrons and dealing with them could be trying. I was one of three resident advisors assigned to the Hall, and the only one to escape any real confrontation with the resident manager. The other two RAs, one Jewish and one Italian, both graduate students, were puzzled by my ability to avoid conflict with her. What they may not have realized was that resolving conflict within a living situation has been ingrained in the Chinese woman's psyche for centuries. Compared to dealing with in-laws, relatives, and concubines, handling a resident manager is hardly much of a problem.

As resident advisor, I shared the duties of manning the office by the front gate, which included chasing away young men at the beginning of curfew hours. Breaking off kissing couples in the lobby was not as easy as chaperoning the social mixer dances, but I took the duties in stride. Panty raids were a happy, hysterical time for the coeds, but not for the resident manager, a nervous and overbearing woman, who was forever afraid of possible disasters. Along with the other two resident advisors, I was to watch our girls closely to prevent any panties being thrown out of the windows. I must confess that I was less than diligent in penalizing the offenders. I was not about to stand in the way of this annual rite of spring.

I got to know the other two RAs well. The three of us rented an apartment for the following summer, as all of us were finishing our master's degrees. I developed a better understanding of the ethnic differences within American culture. The Jewish girl from Boston was high-strung and achievement oriented, whereas the Italian-American girl from Long Island was a devout Roman Catholic, shy, but rich in family support from her relatives back home. We shared our views on womanhood, on the relations between men and women. Despite the progressiveness of the sixties, liberation for women was not a major achievement of the times. We were confused about the role of women and our place in the world.

To some extent, the educational system reinforced our dilemma and the double standard. Even in the School of Social Work, where equality was one of the basic values of our philosophy, the male students were expected to prepare for administrative or managerial positions, regardless of their individual interest, whereas the female students often chose clinical work.

I too was changing. Having rejected my Eastern submissiveness, I was not willing to embrace the Western double standard for women. Nor did I accept the overemphasis put on female physical appearance. I spent four years in college wearing no make-up, and I continued to dress simply and plainly in graduate school.

There were social rituals I learned, to be part of the group. I learned not to get up when a man walked into the room, not to bow to elders, and to address people by their first name right after the first encounter. I even began to understand and to tell some of the off-color jokes.

It was a summer morning when I left Ann Arbor. I had just completed my summer job as Director of the Homemaker Department in the local family service agency, my first administrative position. Having finished packing, I took a last walk across the campus and heard the bells chime from the Bell Tower. I had heard them many times before but never loved them so dearly, nor considered them so full of meaning. Leaving the campus to get married meant the beginning of a new chapter in my life, and moving to Baltimore, Maryland, to start a new job and household, a new challenge. I sat on a park bench next to State Street for the chimes to finish. A young boy, wearing a University of Michigan Wolverine football cap and carrying the bright yellow and blue flag of Michigan walked by. He stopped to give me a good morning.

"Do you live here?" I asked him.

"No, but my dad used to go to school here," he said, proudly.

I thought about my pending departure, and how someday I might come back, with children in tow, who might proudly tell someone that their mother had been a student here.

At that moment, I had no idea that I would miss Ann Arbor as much as I would. Much later, after I had lost the sense of newness in being in this country, the memory of my two years in Ann Arbor would stay with me.

12

A Long Hot Summer

The northern branch of the Detroit YMCA shimmered in the summer heat. Across the street along Woodward Boulevard were single houses, protected by the street's shady trees. I had arrived with one suitcase in hand, accompanied by my host family and now friends, Mary and Jerry, from Ann Arbor, ready to begin my job.

"You'll enjoy our facilities," said the manager pleasantly, a middle-aged woman, formally dressed in a two-piece suit, despite the warm weather. She showed us the gym, pool, and cafeteria before taking us to my room on the fourth floor, a single bedroom equipped with one twin bed, a small desk, chair, and reading lamp. Mary thought I probably could use a small rug to soften the bareness of the room, but she conceded that the room was clean and functional. Mary and Jerry were delighted to help me move to Detroit for the summer.

For me, Detroit was a welcome interlude after a year of graduate study at the University of Michigan. Detroit had been the site of my field work during my first two semesters and I had become familiar with the physical layout of the city. In fact, finding this summer job as a case worker at the International Institute was largely due to the contract I had made through my work with the Family and Children Services of the city Public Welfare Department.

I watched Mary and Jerry drive off in their beige Ford station wagon, leaving behind the stillness of the afternoon street. Traffic was not heavy in this part of the city, and I stood by the door taking in the scenery, realizing I was to spend a whole summer alone in a city far from home for the first time in my life. It was also the first opportunity I would have, without the constant pressure of schoolwork, to reflect on my first year in the United States.

The summer before, I had boarded the China Airline plane at the Taibei airport, waving good-bye to my family and friends. I couldn't wait to start my own adventure. Leaving home for the States had been rehearsed in my mind for a long time.

I knew that had I remained in Taiwan, I would have married soon after finishing college and stayed at home. Or had I continued to work, as I did the first year out of college, my employment options would have been limited, without the intervention of my father. He would have had to use his connections to get me a better job offer, something I would have loathed to have done for me. The prospect of being closely tied to my family was not attractive to me and my urge to break away was further fueled by my desire to go to graduate school.

After sorting out various options, I had passed up the opportunity to study under a scholarship at the East-West Center in Honolulu and had accepted instead a Levi Barbour Scholarship from the University of Michigan, enticed by the lure of entering the mainstream of the North American continent.

My parents supported my wish to study abroad. That I would be traveling with my fiance, whom I had known for two years, was reassuring to them, allaying their fear that I would end up a lonely old maid or, worse yet, marrying a Caucasian.

As I stood on the steps of the Detroit YMCA waving good-bye to Mary and Jerry, I was sadly reminded of my changed relationship with my fiance.

I recalled how I had responded to the courtship. It was largely my sense of vanity. When the most handsome faculty member asked me out, I could not refuse. Later, family, friends, everyone, saw it as the "perfect match." I remember the doubts I had about the differences in our approach to life and our lack of compatibility, but each time my doubts surfaced they were quickly dismissed by my family and my friends as irrelevant trivia. One summer evening, I was asked by my father-in-law-to-be, after a lovely dinner at my fiance's house, whether I had decided upon a date for the engagement. I fumbled for words, and murmured something about discussing it with my parents.

On the day of the engagement, I sat in my room for as long as I could before being taken to the lavish restaurant banquet prepared for the occasion. I was not sure I wanted to go through with the whole thing. Yet another part of me argued that this probably would be as good as most marriages I had known—very few of them could be considered happy.

Arranged marriages were no longer in vogue in Taiwan, but Chinese families could never totally disengage themselves from match-making. Parents and relatives were forever scouting potential mates and hoping the young couple would accept the family's choice. One elderly gentleman whose collection of Chinese antiques could compete with the best in the National Museum in Taiwan, and with whom I shared an interest in art, was insistent that I meet his grandson. A long-distance courtship was arranged by him and I reluctantly accepted a few dates. To my relief, I was able to graciously get out of further entanglements without any of the potential embarrassment there could be for all and without hurting the old man's feelings. I still corresponded with the grandson long after the failed match-making, convinced that our friendship should not be affected.

Terminating my own engagement would not be as easy. I stayed awake the first night in Detroit, trying to sort out the reasons for the demise of a relationship that had lasted for nearly three years. Had I ever approached it from what I wanted, rather than what the people around me wanted? Had I grown more Westernized in one short year at Ann Arbor and become less willing to accept the Chinese notion of a woman's destiny? It might be less painful to go through with the marriage. I knew that breaking the engagement would hurt many people, including my future parents-in-law, of whom I had grown very fond. Was my own happiness more important than that of others dear to me? My Chinese upbringing said no. Yet my first year in the States opened my eyes to many new values, among them, that the individual pursuit of happiness was not shameful.

I started my summer job the next day. The Detroit International Institute was colorful and culturally diversified—most of the staff had come from other countries. Many different languages were spoken at work, particularly when working with the new immigrant group, the primary client group for the Institute's social services and cultural activities. My co-workers ranged from a retired judge from Poland and Ukrainian social worker to an Italian secretary whose shyness around men surprised even someone as sheltered as I was.

Learning about different cultures in a supportive environment was a unique experience for me. I had a caseload of forty to forty-five newly arrived immigrants, each with his or her own difficulties in this new land—physical and mental illness, family problems, and adjustment to a new society. One Romanian lady who had accompanied her husband to America had found herself suddenly a widow with no means of support. I knocked on her door one afternoon, and tried to coax her out to join more activities at the Institute.

Another referral made by the school authorities involved a Chinese-American teenage girl born to a Caucasian woman and a Chinese sailor who had jumped ship to open a restaurant in Detroit. The school reported poor performance academically and a poor attendance record. I made a home visit.

I found this young girl in a small, dirty restaurant, working in the kitchen with her father who spoke a southern Chinese dialect and very little English. The mother had been in and out of inpatient psychiatric care for years, and had not been home to provide adult supervision. The father spoke of his interest in marrying off his daughter to one of his sailor friends, whereas the girl was trying to strike out on her own, having begun an active romance with an Italian-American boy next door.

It was work with the immigrant families that made me more aware of my own adaptation. Every emotional response I had to this new society was magnified by the vivid life experiences of the immigrants I worked with. I discovered that my own adaptation had been faster and easier. In order to help the immigrants I boned up on the literature, including practical tips on surviving on one's own, and I paid more attention to my own surroundings.

From immigrant Chinese families I came to understand the discrimination and prejudice that Chinese in the States still face. The myth about the overseas Chinese making it in the land of gold was quickly dispelled when the reality became clear. For every success story, there are countless failures and shattered dreams.

Yet beyond the ethnic differences, there were common experiences shared by all the ethnic groups I got to know at the Institute. The Polish judge, who had decided to give up his legal career in the States, would drop in to reminisce about his more glorious days as a judge in Poland. "I wanted to die in Poland!" he would pound the table, "And the Communists ruined it for me!" I listened to him, thinking of those Chinese who wanted their ashes to be taken back to their homeland after their death.

Social activities at the Institute blossomed in the evenings, when most cultural events were held. I attended an international ball with a Greek co-worker but declined his invitation to see the city after the dance. Being engaged, from a Chinese point of view, was tantamount to being married. Seeing other men was strictly taboo.

During my first year in Ann Arbor, my Chinese friends insulated me by telling other men that I was engaged. My fiance visited occasionally from another city. I felt indifferent about his visits and equally indifferent toward his absence. I thought it was my preoccupation with school work. We argued a lot when we did see each other. Our adjustments to the States had not moved on parallel courses. I was more adaptive than he, and he was increasingly uncomfortable with my rapid acculturation.

Away from Ann Arbor, I had more time to think about the past year with my fiance. I wrote at night, mostly prose and short stories, and many were being accepted for publication in a leading newspaper in Taiwan. My emotional response to my first year in the States was raw and poignant —good inspiration for my creative energies. The summer heat hit in July. Outside the window beyond the rows of tall city buildings was a sleepy moon, my only companion at night. I found being alone a rare treasure, all secretive and all mine.

Then I met someone who would change my existence for the remainder of the summer. John had come from Pennsylvania and had recently completed his graduate work at a nearby university. He asked me out after meeting me at work. I told him I was engaged and could not go out with any man. Undaunted he responded, "There's no law against your going to a concert with me, is there?"

What started as a perfectly casual, friendly encounter turned into a serious romance a few weeks later. Probably I was ready for a deeper understanding with another person. The difference in cultural background seemed to add to the aura of excitement of getting to know someone well. Oddly enough, I felt no sense of guilt about seeing John— my tie to my fiance had long since been lost. Seeing John also helped me to come to grips with my own needs: I was becoming my own person, slowly but surely. That summer we spent most of our leisure time together.

John took me to see his family and proposed marriage before the summer was over. This was when I began to pull back. As much as I enjoyed our time together, I had not shed all my rational and practical upbringing. I had been conditioned to view marriage differently from romance, and I was not sure that John and I could enter into a more permanent arrangement, given the difference in cultural background and the disapproval I could expect from my family. We had arguments about our different perspectives.

"What else do you want in marriage, Alice, if you have love and respect?" He would ask.

"But you need compatibility," I would say. "You can't depend on romance. Infatuation comes and goes. What would we have after it's gone?"

"I care about now, about you and me." He was desperate.

"Let's wait until the summer is over," I would end the argument, postponing any decision.

Yes, I said to myself, when summer is over. Then I would know for sure. I needed time to sort things out for myself. And I needed to do something about my engagement.

The summer was not yet over when I finally wrote to my fiance to tell him our engagement was over. Whether or not anything would come of my relationship with John, I knew I could not go through with the plan to marry my fiance.

A few days after I sent out the fateful letter to my fiance, he showed up on the doorstep of the Y. Suitcase in hand, he looked distraught and miserable. "Can we talk?" he asked. I was to get his side of the situation, what the break-up would mean to him, to his family, and mine. I listened and felt torn.

Then he gave me the clue to my own role in the dilemma. "Wouldn't you say, Rongrong," he suggested, "that it is far better for a woman to be loved than to love? I shall be good to you. That's security for a woman, isn't it?"

I realized in that instant that I had been conditioned to think about a serious relationship more in terms of security. Wasn't it part of the Chinese woman's goal to secure a permanent "rice bowl" by marrying? Hadn't Mother and her sisters, and all the women of her generation, considered reliability and dependability in a husband the ultimate virtue?

I knew then I would be breaking from my Chinese tradition in a personal and profound way. I would not be content merely with a dependable husband; I preferred to depend on myself. I felt free by coming to this understanding, but I also felt suspended between two cultures.

I sent my fiance off with the assurance that I would wait until the end of the summer. Reluctantly he left. I saw him off, feeling pangs of guilt for the first time. Had I been more honest and courageous, I would have ended the relationship long before this. My own cowardice and inertia had contributed to his unhappiness, and with it, wasted time and energy for both of us. I had no right to hurt him any more.

By now, the ending of the summer was to be the turning point. I would have to reach a number of critical decisions in my life. Summer was getting shorter and longer all at once.

I returned to Ann Arbor in early September, a woman with a changed perspective. Once again, school work occupied most of my time and energy, and I was to begin a new job as the resident advisor in Mosher Hall. I continued to see John for a while. The magic was fading, summer in Detroit a receding memory. The break-up with my fiance became final a few months later, after more painful discussions with him about our lack of a future together. Our parents would be having the same painful discussions at home in Taiwan; the union between a couple in China is always a family affair. I stood firm in my conviction that I would go a separate way. After also telling John we needed to call it quits I was alone again.

A year later, as I was getting ready to marry Nan who, like myself, was a graduate student from Taiwan, I heard again from John, who was about to leave Detroit for the West Coast. I told him I was getting married in two weeks. There was silence on the phone. Then he asked, "Is he Chinese?"

"Yes, he is," I said, waiting for the response from him that I had expected.

"I knew I could always count on the practical side of you." There was resignation in his voice. He recovered and wished me well. Then he said, "It was a good summer, wasn't it?"

"A wonderful summer," I said. "And I had you to thank for it."

CHAPTER

13

The Myth Of the Oriental Woman's Sexuality

There has always been an exotic aura surrounding the sexuality of Oriental women. To the West, the faraway land called the "Orient" was easy to romanticize. Popular novels of the early twentieth century played up the myth.

It is with some shame that I confess how her charm enveloped me like a magic cloud. Unfamiliar with the complex Oriental temperament, I had laughed at Nayland Smith when he had spoken of this girl's infatuation. "Love in the East," he had said, "is like this conjurer's mango tree; it is born, grows and flowers at the touch of a hand." Now, in those pleading eyes I read confirmation of his words. Her clothes or her hair exhaled a faint perfume. Like all Fu-Manchu's servants, she was perfectly chosen for her peculiar duties, her beauty was wholly intoxicating.[2]

Given the lack of direct information to dispel the myths about Oriental women, such half-truths, as in the Fu-

129

Manchu movies and Charlie Chan detective stories, only served to perpetuate the misunderstanding and ethnic stereotyping.

Truth could hurt in a different way. Very few Oriental women wanted to meet the stereotype head on. It was far easier not to challenge the image, however incorrect it might be, than to accept the truth about Oriental sexuality: There is no magic; it is commonplace and quite ordinary, as ordinary as the sexuality of any ethnic group. Moreover, sexuality in Oriental women has remained one of the least explored areas of individual growth and development.

Not long ago I was discussing marital life with a close friend of mine, an educated Chinese woman, who admitted that both she and her husband were so ignorant of the sexual aspects of marriage that they had been married for more than a month before they found out how to make love. Many Chinese women friends, accomplished in the work place, still had no intimate experience as single women with members of the opposite sex. Such isolation and misinformation are common among modern Chinese women, and men, for that matter. The roots of this ignorance lie in the past and they have continued to hinder a more enlightened approach to sexuality.

The birth of a girl was considered a misfortune for the Chinese family. Through continuous conditioning into her relatively low status in the family structure, a young girl was taught to exercise self-denial, which included denial of a sexual self. Segregated from men from the age of seven on, the young girl had very few opportunities for social interaction with members of the opposite sex, except for close male relatives. Then when she married, she had to undergo the psychological trauma of becoming intimate with a man she had not even met, in a marriage arranged by others. A bride-to-be was told by her mother to "tolerate" the first conjugal experience, not to "enjoy" it. Her fear was further increased by the high premium placed on virginity. To demonstrate that his bride was a virgin, the bridegroom was required to show a bloodstained towel the morning after as hard evidence for his family. A marriage could be annulled if the evidence was missing.

Since marriage served the primary function of extending the family, the sexual act itself became strictly utilitarian. The puritanical teaching by Chinese mothers was deficient in basic knowledge about the reproductive organs and how they worked.

Under such cultural and societal constraints, it would take a small miracle to turn Oriental women into sexual beings. Then, why was there such a different view about this most misunderstood thing? Setting aside the West's fascination with the Orient and its people, there was, indeed, a heightened sexuality in a certain strata of Chinese society.

Sexuality had been alive and well in ancient China, particularly in the Tang dynasty, which had a profound impact on Japanese sexual mores as well. Like the "ladies of the pleasures" in Japan, Chinese women have historically placed sexuality outside the bounds of marriage. Literary works of the Tang and Song dynasties praised the beauty and the talent of high-class prostitutes, or "friends" for the male intelligentsia. Married women rarely figured in such works. Sensuality was presumed to be associated with a different class of women whose sole function was to please men, and whose practices, charm, and bedroom techniques were their primary asset in survival.

A "proper" woman would attempt to minimize her sexuality whereas a "loose" woman would flaunt it, even becoming proficient in the arts of love. Yet other Chinese women also recognized the power of female sexuality and its hold on the men who so dominated their lives. The court ladies of the imperial palace knew that losing favor would mean being consigned to the "cold palace," the living quarters for concubines not currently sharing the emperor's attentions, a fate no aspiring court lady desired. Sexuality thus became a tool in the Chinese women's struggle for at least some control over their own destinies.

If one feature sets apart Oriental sexuality from that of the West, it is the relatively natural way that Oriental women approach the sexual act itself. Lacking the concept of "original sin" of the Western religious belief system, Oriental men and women have regarded sex as simply a natural part of living, of interacting with and manipulating the external world. Even the moralistic Confucius acknowledged that "sex is like food," a normal and necessary human activity.

Sex was rarely considered "dirty" in puritanical China. It was only considered shameful if practiced outside the norm. My mother, who taught junior high school, confiscated a nude statue from a student, a replica of Venus, an imported objet d'art. She had discovered that the students, all innocent teenage boys and girls, were using the statue to discuss female anatomy. Mother caught them saying to one another, "Aren't you ashamed of yourself for not having big breasts?" She reprimanded them and hid the statue in her desk drawer. By accident, the statue found its way into the family belongings through many family moves and became part of the furnishings in the house I grew up in in Taiwan. By then, Mother did not care very much about its nudity and was comfortable displaying the statue. It was about this time that nude male and female models started to pose for art classes in Chinese universities in Taiwan. The times were changing slowly.

Modern Chinese women have not moved beyond the traditional teachings of female sexuality. The heroines in the popular movies in Taiwan and in mainland China tend to be virginal, pure and innocent, as opposed to sensual and sexual.

A classmate of mine from Jingshui Middle School in Taiwan who later became a well-known popular singer on the island, was an exception to the rule. Not interested in studies, she expressed a particular liking for Western movies. Marilyn Monroe's *Niagara* had just been shown in the movie theaters in Taiwan. One day I was walking behind her after class when I noticed how well she imitated the Monroe walk: Her hips swinging, she was seductive and provocative. Yet she was also the subject of ridicule as female students dismissed her open sexuality as "cheap" and "improper," and for a long time at school she was a social outcast.

If young women were sheltered and protected, young men in China were equally uninformed and naive, unless fathers took some special pains to educate their sons. In certain parts of China and in certain families, taking the son to a selected brothel was considered a proper way to "initiate" the son before his wedding. This is still practiced today.

A few years younger than my classmates, I went through middle school somewhat oblivious to my classmates' sexual awakening. One afternoon after school I passed a rice paddy on the way home and saw a couple, from the upper-class of my school, in a tight embrace. Embarrassed, I raced on home to tell my mother, who knew the mother of the girl. Mother wisely did nothing, but in the ensuing weeks I heard people in school talking disapprovingly about the budding romance, since dating was not allowed in middle school. The romance eventually ended because of all the outside pressure, despite the fact that both students were in their last year of high school and were ready to graduate. Years later I heard from old schoolmates that they had gone their separate ways into unhappy marriages; but the two eventually were reunited after the failure of their marriages, giving credence to the feelings they had originally shared. Yet the school rules being the way they were, their early romance, if it had continued, would have had a difficult time surviving.

A female teacher of mine seemed to suffer a more repressed life. I first noticed her unusual appearance when she was transferred from a city school to our village middle school. Somewhat weather-beaten, she still retained the good looks of an attractive women. I heard soon after her arrival that she was a single woman who had a questionable reputation with men. In fact, she had had numerous men in her short teaching career, without settling down. The fact that women could date as many men as men did women was never socially acceptable. After failing to ward off public pressure regarding her conduct, she had left the city school to join our school in the village.

My family had moved closer to the middle school and therefore closer to the teachers' residences. After supper, I often walked in the athletic field to get a good view of the sunset.

Late one afternoon, as I walked through the back gate of the school leading to the athletic field, I noticed a woman in a red mandarin dress leaning against the wall surrounding the field. I recognized the new teacher's attire, unusual in the countryside but which was her trademark in school, and I walked over. She was crying silently, with her back toward me, facing the wall.

"Good evening," I greeted her. I had been hesitant to alarm her, but my curiosity had got the better of me.

She turned around, drying her eyes. Against the sunset, her hair glowed and her fading beauty was covered softly in the dusk. She smiled.

"So it's you." She looked at me briefly then quickly turned sideways toward the empty space beyond me. "You probably wonder why I seem so sad," she said to no one in particular. "That's because being a woman is a sad business."

I was fascinated by what she had just said. "I don't understand," I said, and I asked, "Can you explain that?"

She turned her glance to fix on my face for a moment. "You are so young and innocent, Murong," she said, "but someday you'll understand what a burden it is to be a Chinese woman born in this century, when you can't do what a man can do, when you're supposed to be either an old maid with no love interests or a woman married to a bore!"

I stood transfixed. No adult women had ever before talked to me about such things. I dared not move.

"And I choose to be neither!" she exclaimed. "Damn them all."

Not quite grasping her meaning, I knew the best thing for me was to remain silent. We stood in the sunset watching the clouds turning orange, pink, purple, and black, until the first evening star appeared in the darkening sky.

A few months later, she disappeared from the school and never returned, leaving her apartment and all her belongings. Much later I heard that people had seen her walking alone in the street of an adjacent city, looking freer and happier. She remained a mystery to me and to the others, but we suspected that she left to lead the life she had wanted before coming to our village school.

It would always be the daring few who sought to challenge the traditional expectations for Chinese women, who would defy the limitations placed on female sexuality. They would continue to be shunned and misunderstood, for the majority of Oriental women remained confined to the old teaching that proper women should not be sexual. For them, the sexual awakening would come late, if ever.

Part Three

WOMEN OF
LIBERATION — AND
THEIR MEN

14

Fifth Aunt and My Muslim Clan

In 1979, I returned to China for the first time since 1949, the year I left for Taiwan with my immediate family. In these thirty years, so many things seemed to have changed. Rickshaws had been replaced by millions of bicycles, and no longer were there beggars on every street corner. All men and women of working age seemed to have jobs and responsibilities, and they walked or rode down the streets with renewed purpose. Education was now universal, at least for the primary grades, so bands of idle children no longer roamed the streets.

Yes, many things had changed, yet I was also struck by how strong the values of family and human relationships had remained.

I would return in 1982 and 1985, but this first journey was significant. It was a journey to find my roots. I carried my family's mission to locate the many relatives with whom we had lost contact during the thirty intervening years of separation.

Finding the two closest of my relatives, my cousin Zhenli and my fifth aunt, was sheer coincidence. At my mother's urging I had written several letters to the old address in Wuchang, now part of Wuhan, Hubei, where Grandmother Li had lived. I had the dim hope that in the event the Li family no longer lived at the same residence, the new inhabitants would recognize the family I had written to and would forward the letter to the proper address. I wrote to my first aunt, the remaining family matriarch, from the United States, since personal communications between Taiwan and mainland China were not permitted. No response came. Concerned that my letter might have been lost, I wrote again, this time marking on the envelope my relationship with my first aunt and the purpose of my correspondence. Still no response. I then wrote to the Wuhan post office, asking them to forward my letter. After a few tries, I gave up.

Then in 1978, more than ten years after I had stopped trying to locate my relatives, I received not one, but two letters: one from Zhenli in Beijing and one from my fifth aunt in Wuhan. Zhenli explained that while my letters had reached them at the old address where they still lived in Grandmother's house, they had not dared to respond for fear of being labeled as having "overseas connections," a serious crime during the Cultural Revolution. It was not until the normalization of Sino-American relations that the family felt safe enough to write back.

Recovering from my initial shock at hearing from her, I looked at the enclosed photo of Zhenli, a bespectacled, middle-aged-looking woman in a shapeless shirt and pants, with a short, blunt haircut. Any trace of the eight-year-old Zhenli of my memories could not be found. I had to remind myself of the passage of time.

My fifth aunt had more news for me and for Mother in Taiwan, as she was anxious to communicate with Mother through me. She recounted a number of tragic events in the family: the death of Grandmother Li, a couple of years after Liberation; the death of my first aunt, more than ten years later; the disappearance of Lianfeng, son of my first aunt, who had been abducted by an aboriginal tribe during the retreat of the Nationalist Army and his reappearance, only to be sent to a labor camp. Fifth Aunt also mentioned her second marriage, following the death of her police chief husband who had died of illness in prison. Fifth Aunt urged me to visit them in Wuhan.

During the years of our enforced separation from our relatives in China, I had listened to Mother's account of the individual stories of their earlier lives. It was not too difficult for me to piece together the relationships referred to in the letters from Zhenli and my fifth aunt. My reactions to the tragic tales were mixed. I was sad for them, but somewhat protected from direct grief. Even the death of Grandmother Li seemed an event that I had rehearsed in my mind for quite some time—I had got used to our worst fears about their plight. Her passing was almost a relief to me, for it also meant that she had been spared any subsequent suffering during the Cultural Revolution.

Full of excitement, I wrote to Mother in Taiwan that I had accomplished the unexpected contact. I heard from Mother immediately imploring me to make a personal trip to the mainland, something I had been contemplating ever since receiving the letters from Zhenli and my fifth aunt. Thus with help from friends at the China UN Mission, I made the trip in 1979 with my husband, who had similar roots-seeking in mind.

We entered China by train from Hong Kong. The first

railroad station inside China was everything I had imagined: a sparsely decorated waiting room with Chairman Mao's portrait; Red Army soldiers with red stars pinned on their shirt collars; a clean but sterile interview room. The busy throng of overseas Chinese were making their regular trips, laden with TVs, radios, and other goods for their relatives. Their presence was well tolerated by the customs staff. Chinese from the surrounding territories had been making the same journey for years, undeterred by the new government's changing political tides. It was only upon arrival in Guangzhou that I had my first strong reaction to the country I had left thirty years before.

The Guangzhou train station was relatively new and built in the typical Soviet style-high ceiling, big heavy pillars, and square halls. I came out of the train station and was assaulted by the grim landscape of this once-prosperous city: rows of grayish rundown buildings with chipped paint and darkened walls, signs of long neglect; laundry hung between buildings, sometimes outside the front door. Everyone was dressed in white, navy blue, gray, or khaki. Giant posters containing propaganda about the progress of socialism and the greatness of Chairman Mao decorated the streets.

I began to get a severe headache while on the bus going to the hotel. The pain was sharp and blinding and I recognized immediately that it was a reaction to this city, to my father's home province. I had romanticized this ancient land while away from Chinese soil and was having a hard time giving up my illusion. I knew I had to wait out the reaction. After taking some herbal medicine with tea, I lay down on the hotel bed, letting my sadness and disappointment fill me. A couple of hours later the headache was gone.

My recovery was more than physical when, the next

morning, I was awakened by quiet, rhythmic noises outside the hotel window. I went out on the balcony and saw the cyclists riding across the bridge over the Pearl River. Under the window and in the park were people of all ages doing morning exercises. The elderly were doing less strenuous exercises such as Taijiquan and the young people were jogging or running. Something connected me with the people below as if I had been on the same land with them all this time, as if I had never left. It was the same China that I had left more than thirty years before.

I walked the small street along the Pearl River. Against the red banners with slogans hung on the other side of the river, riverboats, ancient junks, and steamboats were moving up and down the stream. By the riverbank was a group of youngsters, out of school on summer vacation, playing and swimming in the yellowish river and having a great time, oblivious to the polluted water and the many boats sailing by. Not far from the bank were elderly citizens playing Chinese chess on the sidewalk, surrounded by bystanders and friends. I was beginning to get the pulse of this city. In spite of the political changes, Guangzhou had maintained its rhythm and order, its distinctive language and history. Returning to the Overseas Hotel where we were staying, I stopped to let a procession of nursery school children go by, singing and laughing, their colorful clothes giving life to the city streets.

I made inquiries about my father's younger sister, whom I had met in Guangzhou in 1948 on our way to Taiwan. But while I knew her maiden name, I could not be sure that she had remained single. I drew a blank with the travel agency. We left Guangzhou for Wuhan.

Our train ride to Wuhan, in my mother's home province of Hubei, was invigorating. Never had I seen such endless rice paddies, on the mountainsides, in the valleys, and on the plains, every inch of cultivable land was being thoroughly used. In the distance I could see the familiar scene of farmers with their water buffalo. Some of the farmers were women, working the fields like the men. I thought about my grandmother Pu who had once worked on the land, tending her vegetable garden. I thought about her children, most of them long gone except for my father and the aunt I could not locate. I wondered if Father had kept the same farm scene in his memory. I was sure he had, for no one could be indifferent to the Chinese countryside.

I had written to my fifth aunt about our arrival time in Wuhan. Not knowing the transportation arrangements, I had also requested the China Travel Agency to pick us up at the station. But as I stepped out of the train I was immediately greeted by shouts in the local Wuhan dialect, "Rongrong! Is that you?" I turned and saw three eager faces: two young men and a woman, all in their twenties, were approaching me. From photos sent to me before the trip I recognized them as my cousins, children of my fifth aunt. Also approaching me, a few feet away, was a short, plump elderly woman, walking slowly and with some difficulty. She broke out in a smile, the same smile that had dazzled my fifth uncle, the police chief, so many decades ago. I went over to hug her exclaiming, "Fifth Aunt!" She smiled and hugged me, saying, "So you are Rongrong. You have indeed grown." After a round of introductions there was some confusion about who should be riding with whom. But all was quickly resolved as my new fifth uncle had miraculously arrived with a borrowed van. Together with the van from the travel agency, we set out for the Hankou part of Wuhan city.

My fifth aunt had moved to Hankou when she married

her first husband. It was in Hankou that she started working as an accountant for an import division of the Hubei provincial government, a position she never left. I was surprised by the stability of her employment, given the many upheavals in the political situation. I was told that while Fifth Aunt's connection with the Nationalist government through her police chief husband had put her in a difficult position, his death in jail had more than compensated for her not-so-pure political background, and that individuals with skills and only minor political problems were valued by the government.

At Fifth Aunt's insistence, we stayed only one night at the local hotel and moved in with her family the next day. The news about our arrival had reached the other clan members and soon the house was swarming with well-wishers and relatives that I had never met nor even heard of. Even though I was familiar with this typical Chinese hospitality, the warmth and reception by all was still overwhelming. I instantly became the family ambassador from overseas with the mission to fill in the gaps of their knowledge about life outside China.

The most striking impression I formed as I met each clan member was the way my Muslim clan looked. I had some knowledge of my own Muslim lineage, but since Father was non-Muslim and we children never practiced the religion at home, I had never given it much thought. But the differences in physical characteristics were remarkable: curly hair, high nose-bridge, somewhat paler complexion, and deep-set eyes. Had they been dressed differently, they could easily pass as Middle Easterners. I was also struck by the difference in food. The non-pork cuisine is popular with non-Muslim Chinese as well, for its more vigorous adherence to sanitary rules and its lighter, healthier diet.

One member of this expanding family especially caught my attention: the son of my second aunt's sister-in-law, who had been the only woman of the family ever to attend medical school. Her son was now working as a cab driver—a lean, tall, somewhat shy young man with not much memory of his own famous mother. She had died when he was still very young. But he had a full grasp of all the family relationships. He was curious about his mother's extended family and kept asking me questions about my own mother, who had been close to his mother, both being about the same age.

The impact of the Cultural Revolution could best be seen in my fifth aunt's family. All of her five children had been unable to finish high school because of the interruption of classes. Her eldest son was sent to a rural community to do farm work, leaving his high school education unfinished. The second son had rebelled against any adult discipline and had joined a youth gang. He had been in and out of jail since then. The three children from her second marriage had not fared well either. All had had their schooling interrupted and terminated, and all had become Red Guards. They recounted their days of wandering in the countryside, riding the trains free—the Red Guards had had unlimited transportation privileges—and taking free meals and lodging in any city they visited, waving Mao's red book. Their life on the road had become boring after a while and they soon missed the structure of home and school, but all regular schools had been closed during the Cultural Revolution. In those that remained open, the curriculum had been changed to political teaching exclusively. Fifth Aunt's only daughter said the one thing she had got from the Cultural Revolution was learning how to cook, which she had taken up out of sheer boredom and the lack of meaningful activities at home or in school.

Near the end of the Cultural Revolution, my cousins had tried to return to school. Unfortunately they had had such a poor educational foundation that they could no longer compete with the younger students fresh out of high school for the college entrance exams. Additionally, the current Chinese policy of not admitting anyone over twenty-five into college militated against them.

But despite their struggles, I sensed a feeling of optimism among my cousins. Instead of being defeated, each of them had pursued learning on his own. The most popular present I brought was a tape recorder, which they promptly used to record English lessons. The traditional value placed on education and learning had not been destroyed by the Cultural Revolution after all.

During our short stay at Hankou I also met Mingqiong, my cousin, daughter of my second aunt, mother's second eldest sister. I remembered her slightly, only because her name had been romantically linked with Lianfeng, son of my first aunt. Mingqiong was now married to a journalist, an outspoken, vivacious man who was working on the social problems of Hankou and who covered current affairs for the local newspaper. Their two daughters were more representative of the youngest generation of Chinese. Free from the scars of the Cultural Revolution, they seemed more pragmatic about their future and talked mainly about the same kind of issues that concerned their Western counterparts, such as boyfriends, school, and jobs. Mingqiong had been sent to North Korea to fight in the Korean War where she had contracted an illness that damaged her spine and hipbones. She walked slowly and painfully with the aid of a cane. In her early forties, she was already aged.

She reminisced about her life with us in Chengdu and about her work as a middle school student before Liberation.

We went to see an old late-fifties movie together, a love story that had been banned during the Cultural Revolution for its "decadent" influence on the young. Sitting in the theater, I heard the eager response and excitement of the young audience. They could have been teenagers of any culture.

I found my fifth aunt very different from Mother. Where Mother was outspoken and direct, Fifth Aunt was soft, retiring, and gentle. She laughed at my comparison of her to Mother and told me that she had always been afraid of my mother's temper. Her current husband, my fifth uncle, was a stern, self-centered man who seemed to take her for granted. He had grown up in the pre-Liberation era and still kept the old male attitudes toward the family. The roles in my fifth aunt's home were sharply divided. Fifth Uncle, as head of the family, was to be waited on by wife and children. Women of my fifth aunt's generation, even in the new China, still carried the heavy burdens of home while holding full-time jobs outside. Yet my fifth aunt accepted this arrangement as more humane than the treatment her own sisters had received in their lifetimes.

Fifth Aunt was now the surviving family matriarch in the Li family, succeeding my first aunt in this role. Unlike my first aunt, she ruled the family in her quiet, conciliatory manner. Like my first aunt, however she was selfless and loyal to the Li family.

After a two day stay, I found it difficult to say good-bye. I would have liked to find out more about my fifth aunt, the Li family, and Grandmother Li. I would have liked to visit Grandmother Li's house but Wuchang city was still some distance away and changing my travel itinerary would have been difficult. I vowed to return at a future date.

The day of our departure, the entire Li family clan wanted to walk us to the railroad station. Fifth Aunt also insisted on walking despite her back problem.

Dusk had set in. The street was full of people returning home from work. Several blocks from the train station I saw a woman walking toward us, holding the hand of a little girl. The woman looked impoverished even in the midst of the plain-dressed people. Her hair was dishevelled, her face dirty, and she wore a heavy jacket even in the August heat. I inquired about their origin and destination and was told that they were most likely refugees from Henan province, escaping the yearly famine. All of a sudden an early childhood memory flashed back: I saw the Henan woman with her little girl in the boat shed on the Nanjing docks where my infant brother, Mother, and I had waited before leaving for Wuhan.

I turned around to look at my fifth aunt, her hair graying and her face wrinkled. I remembered the young, blushing bride for whose wedding I had been the flower child, more than thirty years ago. We had kept living as best we knew how—China and the family with whom I had been reunited —our survival instinct as strong as ever.

15

Cousin Lianfeng— Soldier and Slave

I saw cousin Lianfeng again after thirty-three years, in the city of Chengdu, Sichuan province, in the summer of 1982. I spent four days with him. Trying to fill in the blanks of all those lost years, I found myself in a world both familiar and alien.

I had been a small child when my parents, my infant brother, and I left China in 1949. I could recall the relatives left behind only from old photo albums, from Mother's painful and broken accounts during her rare nostalgic moments, and from a few of my own disjointed childhood memories. These memories are of a courtyard, a plum tree in winter, a fish pond, the displeasure on my first aunt's face after I had won a fist fight with my cousin Zhenli, who though three years my senior often lost fights with me and cried easily.

I remember Lianfeng as a tall, handsome officer, always dressed in an immaculate uniform and army boots (at least whenever he visited us in Nanjing). To me he was amazingly strong for he could lift me over his head and spin me around and around until I pleaded, "Stop! Stop! I've had enough!" Afterwards, we would ride in my father's shiny new jeep to Zhongshanling, the Memorial Tomb for Dr. Sun Yat-sen in the suburbs of Nanjing, where I would race everyone up the 299 steps leading to the entrance of the tomb. Naturally, they always dragged behind to let me win. I was the carefree child in a family surrounded by indulgent adults.

The image of Lianfeng in his shining army boots stayed with me during the ensuing years. I heard, much later when I was in my teens, that he had suffered great hardship, captured by an aboriginal tribe in the southwest of China and held for ransom. The ransom money, sent from central China where Lianfeng's mother, my first aunt, lived, had been kept by a middleman. My mother feared that Lianfeng might have perished in the mountains. Her thoughts of him often ended with a sigh, "What a man and what a waste!"

Before my trip to China in 1982 I had made several inquiries through my relatives on the mainland about Lianfeng. He was still alive, but since no one from the family had visited him in recent years I received very little information about him other than the fact that he was alive and well, working as a farmer in a small Sichuan village in southwestern China. With Lianfeng's address in hand, I telegraphed him from Wuhan, where I was teaching at a summer institute, and asked him to meet me in Chengdu city.

The flight took close to five hours with one rest stop at Chongqing, the city where my family had stayed for a brief time during the Sino-Japanese War and where the Nationalist government had spent the second half of the war before moving to Taiwan. From the plane I could see the endless rice paddies layered on the mountainsides, green and lush against the dark red earth under the China sky. I saw myself once again as a little girl chasing after butterflies and grasshoppers in the fields. I felt myself gradually being sifted through an invisible rice sieve, leaving out the Western particles accumulated over my long years away from the Chinese soil. I wondered what I would find in Chengdu.

My telegram had not been very specific. I could not tell Lianfeng where I would be staying because the China Travel Agency in Wuhan had left all the local arrangements to the Chengdu agent who would only tell me upon my arrival. If I couldn't see Lianfeng, I consoled myself, I would stay in Chengdu, my birth place, for a few days to do some sightseeing and then move on to Xian, my next stop.

I reminded myself of another mission I had from cousin Mingqiong, who had been Lianfeng's fiance before his captivity. She had come to me in Wuhan to ask me to be her go-between and talk to Lianfeng on her behalf. She wanted Lianfeng to know why she had, without his prior knowledge or consent, married someone else. "You must tell him I did it because I had no other choice," she said with tears in her eyes. "I was sent to the war zone in North Korea, alone and far away from home with no one to turn to. I met my present husband in the army." Mingqiong was in her mid-forties now, a plump woman with a shy demeanor. I tried to picture her as a slip of a girl, infatuated with Lianfeng, the handsome officer. I was touched by her genuine emotion as she went on, "I wanted to reach him before I decided to marry, but no one in the family could locate him. I thought he was dead."

"But I'm sure he'd understand. Many things happened during those years," I said, trying to be helpful.

"I just want him to know I didn't do it because my feelings for him had changed," Mingqiong said, drying her tears on a dark blue handkerchief that matched her blue

Mao jacket. I fell silent. It was not easy to understand why it was necessary to explain a decision made by a young girl so many years before. I knew it mattered much to Mingqiong that I relate the message to Lianfeng. I promised her I would write to her from Chengdu after my talk with him.

The plane landed at Chengdu airport, a newly constructed airfield. Seeing no one waiting for me, I went to the lobby, somewhat dazzled by the newness and whiteness of the marbled walls. A small gift shop and a new information desk filled the center, contributing to the appearance of emptiness in the high-ceilinged room. A young woman came toward me from behind the information desk. With a pleasant smile, and wearing a crisp white cotton blouse and long dark blue pants, she asked in the local dialect about my destination in the city. I smiled broadly and responded: in the old familiar dialect! And I could still speak it.

My ride to the city with my guide—also a young woman with a businesslike manner, who had finally appeared, apologizing for having got the wrong flight schedule— brought back more memories of the ancient city. As our Japanese Toyota passed through the green rice paddies and vegetable fields, I was overwhelmed by the onslaught of the familiar scent of summer vegetables and human waste that were very much part of the scenery of the Chinese countryside. Listening to the facts and statistics cited by my guide about the development of Sichuan province, I thought about the many people who have lived on this land and who will go on growing rice and vegetables in the midst of the new factories and their chimneys. And I would be coming home again and again to pay homage to the underlying simplicity of life and living. I thought about the meaning of a homeland. For years I had carried my roots with me wherever I went, roots mostly cultural and psycho-logocal. Riding through the once-familiar countryside, I knew without a shred of doubt that I was finally home.

I checked into the Jinjiang Hotel, the largest in town, a huge structure built in the fifties for businessmen and officials. My room was comparatively spacious with a large double bed, two big easy chairs, a coffee table and a night stand. The room extended out to a small patio facing the front entrance of the hotel. I had gone out onto the patio to get a bird's-eye view of the city when the phone rang. It was the receptionist: "Are you Murong Pu?" I said yes, wondering what could be the matter. "There's someone at the desk waiting to see you. He gave his name as Lianfeng." "Lianfeng? Why, that's my cousin. I'm coming right down." I was overjoyed. How in the world did Lianfeng find me and only minutes after my arrival?

I ran to the reception room by the front gate of the hotel and saw from a distance an old man standing in the center of the room with his back toward me. Hearing my footsteps he turned around and looked my way. Since he was the only man in the room I had no doubt it was my cousin. I slowed down and tried to remember the impressions of a five-year-old girl. The army uniform was replaced by a gray shirt and shapeless dark green trousers, the shining army boots by a pair of brown plastic sandals. The erect posture had disappeared. I saw a man half bent over with a stooped back; he seemed only about my height. But his face—it was all there, behind the bronzed skin and layered wrinkles—and the eyes were the same, shining and smiling. He was looking at me directly with the beginning of a smile. I ran toward him.

"Lianfeng?"

"Yes, yes, you must be Rongrong." Rongrong was my

childhood nickname. Thank God his voice was almost the same. But other than the smile, he did not move. I had the urge to hug him but quickly caught myself. Instead, I held out my hand and said, "It's so good to see you, Cousin Lianfeng.

It was close to six in the evening. I asked him if he had had supper. Lianfeng said he had already eaten and would like to sit down somewhere to talk. I took him to my room, passing curious bystanders in the lobby, noticing some slight discomfort on his part. True to form, Lianfeng did not say anything to give away his emotions. The silent walk gave me the opportunity to have a better look at him.

He must have been close to sixty (he later told me he was fifty-nine) although he appeared years older. His hair had turned completely gray, but was cropped very close to his head in a short crew cut. He was carrying a black plastic business tote bag, the kind seen often on the streets of China. He rarely made direct eye contact with me even when he was responding to questions about how he had located me so soon and where he was staying in the city. I had never noticed this about him, but, then, it was a long time ago when I knew him. Later he told me he had borrowed the plastic bag from his eldest son, an official in the local commune, just for the trip. He had also borrowed the gray shirt he had on. "I don't own any shirts. You don't need to wear a shirt when you work in the rice fields," he added matter-of-factly.

We talked in the small hotel room sitting across from each other, a coffee table between us. It was beginning to get dark outside. When I could no longer see his face I got up to turn on the lights and suggested a snack. Unfortunately, the dining room was closed by now, so I bought two cans of lukewarm Five-star beer from the gift shop downstairs, and two bags of peanuts. We talked. Mostly he talked and I listened.

Like a summer stream stirred by the wind, Lianfeng was becoming more eloquent and emotional in his account of the last thirty-three years. Occasionally he paused for a moment, taking out a dark blue checkered handkerchief to blow his nose, smiling slightly at me and asking, "Am I boring you with this?" "Oh, no, of course not. Please go on." I would reply.

I was able to piece together an amazing, even triumphant, account from him. Lianfeng had suffered and aged but his spirit remained young and free.

It was 1949. Lianfeng had just left his fiance Mingqiong in Chengdu to rejoin the Nationalist Army. The troops retreated into the high mountains bordering Tibet. They became completely lost and their supplies were running out. They were down to a mere hundred men and as time went on, only a few dozen. Two months after they had started into the mountains they came upon a deep and deserted valley where they were surrounded and captured by the Yi aborigines. Lianfeng was with his lieutenant major when this occurred. The major committed suicide on the spot, using his own handgun. Lianfeng did not and was captured. In later years he thought about his decision not to kill himself. "I did not think much at the time about whether to do it or not. I just knew I still wanted to live and be reunited with my family." Lianfeng was given to an Yi family as a house slave.

In those days the tribe lived very primitively, untouched by the Chinese around them. The Yi were primarily mountain people living at high altitudes, five thousand feet or more above sea level. For centuries they had led an independent existence under the changing regimes in central China.

The family that Lianfeng worked for had one old man and one young girl in her late teens. There, miles away from his home and culture, Lianfeng began his four-year career as a slave to an aboriginal tribe.

The day started early for the mountain people. Up before dawn, Lianfeng would carry a bamboo basket on his back to go picking in the field. More skilled men would trap game, but Lianfeng's job was limited to carrying home the meat. The young girl from the house would go along to help him with his basket. Despite his youth, Lianfeng could not compete with the Yi people in stamina, women included. The loads of more than one hundred pounds were simply beyond him. So Lianfeng quite happily let the young girl help, her only reward being his singing love songs to her in the Han dialect.

"How very romantic!" I exclaimed.

"Well, it certainly helped my own homesickness to have the extra attention." There was a twinkle in his eyes.

Winter in the mountains was long and hard. There were few ways to keep out the cold. Lianfeng slept on the dirt floor in a barn-like dwelling and had only one blanket to ward off the cold when going out. At night he kept his feet warm in dried hay. Despite extreme caution, Lianfeng contracted typhoid fever the following year. With little medical help available, the mountain people usually put the sick out in the open to die a natural death. Lianfeng was carried out to the hill behind the house where he stayed and there he was alone in the open field to fend for himself. He stayed feverish and delirious for two days and two nights, believing that his end was in sight. However, on the third day his fever broke. The master of the house dropped by to check on him and saw his improved condition, so Lianfeng was carried back home to recuperate. The young girl nursed him to health, sharing a better quality of food with him including a piece of lard saved for her own wedding day.

After that, he tried to escape several times, but each time he was caught and brought back by the tribesmen and sold to a different family. Given the lack of transportation and the distances between each mountain household, he lost contact with his old master and the girl he had cared for. In 1959 when the Communists liberated the Yi tribe, Lianfeng was allowed to leave with the Communist army.

This did not represent a turn of luck for Lianfeng who was immediately sent to a labor camp in exchange for his rescue from captivity. Lianfeng's long and previous connection with the Nationalist Army made him a prime target for reform through labor, a system established to rehabilitate those with prior affiliations with the Nationalist government and its armed forces. Lianfeng was assigned to a camp which produced sugar from sugar cane. He worked in the refinery for the next twenty years, eighteen hours a day. In 1979, with the end of the Cultural Revolution, he was made a farmer in a small Sichuan village.

Lianfeng did not have much to say about his work camp experience except for his eternal gratitude to have left the mountains. The day the Communist army arrived he was found to be incoherent in his use of the Chinese language, his health was in jeopardy, and he had lost more than fifty pounds. While working in the refinery he learned, with limited technical knowledge at his disposal, how to measure the various grades of fine sugar. With little resentment at his lost youth and health, Lianfeng said, "I'm reasonably healthy now. I have enough food to feed my family. What more do I need?"

Through an arrangement made by a mutual acquaintance, Lianfeng married a local woman, the former wife of a landlord. Three adult children came with this marriage, and one son was the product of this union, who unfortunately has a congenital defect and is severely retarded and epileptic. All four children and his wife are illiterate. Lianfeng feels that his family life is peaceful and serene and that his role as educator and mediator in his family is satisfying.

At this point I brought up Mingqiong's request that I tell him how she came to marry someone else. I described for him her present life with her journalist husband and two teenage daughters. When I was through, Lianfeng was silent for a long time. Then he spoke.

"Mingqiong was such a young girl then. Of course she was free to marry anyone she wanted. I was the one to blame for leaving her unattended in a strange city."

"But didn't you think of her during all the years you were apart?" I pressed, somewhat puzzled by his unemotional response. Lianfeng again was quiet. He finally turned toward me with a thoughtful look and said, "We grew up together. That's all."

I bit my tongue. It had all of a sudden dawned on me that I had crossed the boundaries between generations, for Lianfeng still belonged to the older generation for whom any outward expression of one's feelings, particularly between men and women, was considered crude and in poor taste.

"But," he spoke again, sensing my embarrassment, "you can tell her that I should be the one to feel bad about the pain she endured, and," his voice grew softer, "I'm so glad she is happily married now." Lianfeng reached for his handkerchief and blew his nose.

The sound jolted me back to reality. Darkness had long since descended. Beyond the small patio I saw the city lights of Chengdu. It is a new city now, trying to regain the vigor and order lost during the Cultural Revolution. Lianfeng was so much like this land, full of scars and wounds, and yet he also understood the wisdom of waiting. Wait and your life will be better. Wait, wait for ten years, twenty years, thirty years. Time can heal anything, anything at all.

The next day he and I toured the city together on foot. We visited the central park area. Lianfeng told me that the park had been renovated in recent years and is now much used by the general public. I nodded, watching the throngs of local people, the elderly, men and women, and the children in their colorful outfits and hats strolling and running down the garden lanes in the park. I saw the ice cream stands stationed side by side, and the tea pavilion where people can go to sip their hot, fragrant tea and crack the seeds of watermelon, pumpkin, and most popular of all during this season—sunflower seeds. Lianfeng showed me a monument in honor of the railroad strike in protest of the foreign influence in China long before Liberation. "Your mother would remember this monument," he said. "It was here when she last visited this park." A few streets away Lianfeng wanted to show me the "old Chengdu" as it had been in the past. "Even the names of the streets remain the same in some parts of the city." he added.

I walked the old streets with him taking care to avoid the potholes and exposed pipes. A few bikes went by, stirring up the dirt on the road. Lianfeng had moved ahead of me by now. I stopped to watch his stooped back and marvelled at his agile movements. I could see him working in the rice fields or carrying a food basket to his working wife or walking from one paddy to another, checking on the progress of his rice seedlings, barebacked and barefooted. My childhood memory of a handsome officer is gone now, replaced by a resilient and brave old man, triumphant and undefeated, far more handsome than the young man I once knew as a little girl.

I got to know him a bit more during the next three days we were together. His silent pride in his piece of land and his family is strong, undiminished by the hardships he had endured and the youth he had lost forever. Lianfeng did not want to dwell on the last thirty-three years. He was more interested in explaining the new adult education project he had taken on for the village and even debated with me the wisdom of the British actions in South America.

The day I left for Xian, he came to the train station to see me off. I asked what I could do for him. "There is one favor I would like to ask of you," he quickly responded, much to my surprise, for he had been totally reticent for the past four days about asking for anything. "I need your help to fight the battle to keep the chemical plant from polluting our village."

I found out from his account that for the last eight years the villagers had been fighting to keep the chemical waste from being dumped into the only river that flows through the village, the only source of water supply for the one thousand and eight hundred villagers and their cattle stock. But the effort to move the chemical plant had fallen on deaf ears because of the national push to give priority to the Four Modernizations movement.

"Perhaps when you get to Beijing you can talk to the right people about this. They may pay more attention to suggestions from an outsider." Lianfeng wrote down the information about the company and the village. I watched him scribbling and tried hard to get rid of the lump in my throat. I told him I would do my best.

We were walking to the platform where the train was waiting. Lianfeng tugged my sleeve slightly and asked again, "Rongrong, I do have another question for you." I stopped, thinking to myself this must be the parting message.

"I want you to tell me, since you have had training in Western psychology," he said, a bit shyly, "whether I'm normal and have all my wits. I did wonder about my own sanity after I left the mountains."

I picked up both of his hands—big, strong, and full of calluses. "Listen, Lianfeng," I said earnestly, "You are the sanest person I have ever met."

He gave me such a broad smile, it was almost childlike. That smile and the image of Lianfeng standing with his stooped back on the platform stayed with me during my long train ride to Xian.

16

A Block Worker in Shanghai

While growing up in Taiwan, I had formed an unfavorable impression of the mainland Communist Chinese neighborhood workers. The anti-Communist propaganda had labeled them as the "listening-to-the-wall gang," meaning people who eavesdrop for the Communist Party officials, directly violating individual privacy and decency. Later in the United States when I began to read about the neighborhood associations, I wondered about their powerful potential for quite another purpose: a grassroots organization for the most effective mutual help efforts in the local community service network. Still, I had no personal experience with either the people or the associations to validate my changing impressions.

In 1979 when I visited Beijing for the first time as part of my reunion with my cousin Zhenli and other relatives in northern China, I took some time out to explore the social and political systems in modern China. I and my husband made some inquiries through the Chinese

Academy of Social Sciences. My husband, a professor of sociology at the State University of New York at Albany, had a strong interest in making contact with the Chinese academic community. We both were invited to give a couple of lectures on U.S. sociological and social welfare trends. As I spoke on the professionalism of the human service professions in the United States, I also mentioned the emerging role of the informal network, a theme that got immediate and spontaneous acknowledgement from scholars in the Academy. They urged me to take a closer look at the basic community organization, the neighborhood structure, and the vital role the block workers play. I agreed and began to make arrangements to do so.

As is typical of most activities in China, things worked out most efficiently through informal channels. I soon learned, by simply mentioning my interest, that a friend of Zhenli could introduce me to her mother, a retired teacher and an active member of a street organization in Shanghai, where we would be visiting next. This friend went so far as to suggest that she could ask her mother to meet me directly at the Shanghai hotel where we would be staying. I thought this a much better way to study the neighborhood association than making official arrangements, and gratefully accepted her offer.

Zhenli's friend was as good as her word. Soon after we arrived in Shanghai, her mother called me at the hotel and we made arrangements to meet the next day.

Meanwhile, we put on comfortable clothes, and carrying the typical tourist camera and bag, went for a walk. Shanghai—the mysterious and the insidious—would never lose its charm. Even with their gray facades, the city's buildings still exuded an old-world glamour. The big clock near the Shanghai harbor was still there, having chimed continuously all these intervening years for a city that had lost its once-exotic inhabitants. I looked in awe at the clock, with the realization that I was actually standing at Shanghai harbor, with all its glamorous and sinful past.

The people moved faster here, were quicker to make contact with visitors, and the merchants were still adept at attracting business. I watched the slim, attractive Shanghai women walk by. Without any doubt, the women here were more feminine than elsewhere in China. It showed in the way they carried themselves and the way they walked.

We went into a department store that catered to the local citizens and saw a more abundant supply of goods than in other cities we had visited on this tour. Television sets had recently begun to be manufactured in factories in Shanghai, and sets of various sizes were the hottest item in the store. One young man, standing at the counter where the TV sets were on display, had grown impatient with the slow pace of the salesperson: "I've got my money in my hand. Do you want to make a deal or not?" the nonchalant reply was, "So do other people. Wait your turn." Accustomed to the eager, aggressive sales approach in the United States, I found this an interesting reversal of roles. But it was fully understandable because sales clerks received no bonus for making a sale and there was a shortage of desirable goods.

On the way out of the department store we were approached by a polite youth. With books in his hands, he appeared to be a college student. He asked where we were from and what had brought us to the city, and when told we were from the United States he immediately suggested some points of interest in Shanghai. Then very politely he asked if he could accompany us to our hotel so we could chat on the way. He was curious about the city and its pre-Liberation past. He was also curious about life outside

168

China, the same curiosity we would encounter again and again on our tour of China. At the hotel door he wanted to exchange his fountain pen for our ballpoint, not a fair trade for him for we were carrying inexpensive ballpoint pens. But he insisted, wanting something from the United States.

Mrs. Zhang, the block worker and mother of Zhenli's friend, showed up at the hotel the next afternoon with her son and his girlfriend. All three of them were small and slim, with delicate features and cultivated manners. We sat in the hotel restaurant and talked.

Mrs. Zhang was now in her late sixties. She had recently retired from a full-time teaching post as a middle school teacher in the Shanghai school system. Her current duties in the neighborhood association included conducting an adult education class and being mediator for the one hundred or so families within her block. As the block leader, elected by the neighborhood, she must be intimately familiar with the individual lives of all the families in the neighborhood. The duties ranged from settling disputes among family members to acting as a Party-appointed implementor of certain policies affecting the neighborhood, usually associated with public health issues. Not too long before, she had been responsible for inspecting the physical condition of each household. The regular street cleaning was enthusiastically and cooperatively carried out. The adult education class she taught was a new program for her block, established at her urging.

As Mrs. Zhang spoke I watched her lively expression and obvious interest in her work. She did not consider herself retired, for her present duties were even more hectic and demanding than her previous responsibilities as a teacher. Her children had left home years before and she had no time to worry about their lives, given her own full-time activities. Her pension as a retired teacher would be about 70 percent of her salary, an incentive for most retirees to work as volunteer neighborhood workers, since living expenses were paid and the work did not affect one's benefits.

The street organization was democratic. The block leader ruled by persuasion, not fiat. Once in office the block leader relied on the traditional Chinese family structure to move the organizational agenda forward. This meant getting accepted as a member of each family before any real official directive could be implemented. Mrs. Zhang recounted her own initial efforts at gaining the confidence of her block families. Only after they were assured of her sincerity did she get their full cooperation.

I watched the interaction between Mrs. Zhang and her son as she related her experience with the street organization. The familiar filial respect and deference in the Chinese family was evident with the Zhangs. I asked Mrs. Zhang whether the transition from teacher to neighborhood worker had been difficult. She replied that it had been quite easy and that she was comfortable in her new role because she treated all the families in her block as her own, with care and compassion. She had one other child who was a friend of Zhenli, with whom she maintained regular contact. Her son worked in the Children's Theater in Shanghai and her daughter was the artistic director of a major dance company in Beijing.

I asked her if some of her activities could be perceived by the families as invasions of their privacy. She denied it, emphasizing the interest and the intent of the program. "When I inquire about marital discord between husband and wife, it is because the mother-in-law or someone else in the family has complained to me about the disharmony in the household," she explained. "I go in and persuade the couple to be on better terms. They may not always welcome my inquiry, but they understand my role as the block leader and the importance of how they are perceived as a family by others." The combination of using extended kinship, group pressure, and community support contributed to the success of the program.

While visiting Zhenli in Beijing I noticed that she had no qualms about asking for assistance from her neighbors to baby-sit for her while she was out doing errands for the family. She would reciprocate with similar favors. Even more impressive was the volunteer help. Soon after we arrived on the scene, Zhenli accepted several offers from her neighbors to cook special dishes for us. Some brought live chickens and ducks for the feast. Others brought their own special recipes already cooked.

The block leader looked out for the protection of the elderly and the infirm. Abuse or allegation of abuse was quickly responded to. Mrs. Zhang had one sobering thought to share: "For centuries the Chinese family regarded as sacrosanct its own activities inside the confines of the home. No more. It's now everyone's business to see to it that all citizens receive fair and humane treatment." I remembered the stories I had heard as a youngster about wife and child abuse, and the typical male response, "My family's my property. I do what I want with them."

I saw a play in Beijing that summer about a block worker. It was a comedy showing how the awkwardness of the block worker's intervention was dealt with by a family determined to reject any outside advice. The audience laughed with recognition; the play had touched a responsive chord. But I had been puzzled by the significance of the production. Was the work of the street organization important enough for dramatization? As I sat there now, listening to Mrs. Zhang's many examples of direct intervention as a block worker in a typical neighborhood, I began to understand the impact this system has made on the basic functioning of the family in modern China. In more ways than one, it has transformed the old closed family system to one open to outside scrutiny—a powerful transformation indeed.

Mrs. Zhang took us for a walk. She talked about how joining the street organization had changed her own outlook on life. "I didn't retire—I went into more active service." She pointed out that any elderly person could take a similar role in the community, and be valued and revered.

Mrs. Zhang left us with her son, as she had to attend another neighborhood meeting that afternoon. Mr. Zhang asked if we wanted to go somewhere else. I indicated an interest in seeing the Friendship Store—visiting the Friendship Store in every city had become part of the routine for most tourists—and he quickly obliged.

Mr. Zhang did not go in with us to the Shanghai Friendship Store, as local people were not admitted at that time. I was bothered by the inequity and was about to go see the manager, but Mr. Zhang stopped me by asking me a favor. He asked if I would purchase one of those locally made television sets for him. He had saved enough money but could not locate a suitable set in the local department store. I recalled the crowd in the store we had visited the day before, and agreed.

This settled, we went into the store and had the TV, a black-and-white nineteen-inch set, sent to Mr. Zhang's apartment. He thanked us profusely. That evening Mr. Zhang arranged for us to get tickets to see *Swan Lake*, performed by the Shanghai Ballet Company, a superb production showing the long and significant tradition of ballet training in China.

The next day we were ready to leave Shanghai for Nanjing where we would be searching for more of our lost relatives. Early in the morning, as we were packing to check out of the hotel, the buzzer rang from the reception desk. It was Mrs. Zhang to see us. I assumed she was there to say good-bye and was touched by her courtesy.

I found her in the lobby downstairs, pacing the floor, looking somewhat impatient. Otherwise, she looked as cool and in control as she had the day before. As soon as she saw me she walked toward me. "I want to apologize," she said. "I had no idea that my son would trouble you with his request to purchase the TV for him. He should have waited his turn at the local department store."

I was relieved to learn the source of her mood and responded, "Oh, that. Don't mention it. He paid for the TV and I was glad to be of help."

She was still hesitant. Then I added, "Besides, I met your daughter in Beijing. She had been very kind toward my cousin Zhenli. You know, she even brought a live hen for our supper the day we arrived."

Mrs. Zhang was visibly relaxed. She said, "Well then, I must still apologize for my son. Have a good journey." She extended her hand and I took it.

I watched her walk out the lobby door. She strode briskly, all businesslike, no doubt headed for some neighborhood business. As I stood there I thought about my first aunt who had also become an active neighborhood worker and had been elected block leader during her final years. I could almost see First Aunt walking from door to door to care for the needy. With her imposing physical appearance, my first aunt must have made a strong impression on her neighborhood families. I suddenly felt closer to Mrs. Zhang and to what she was attempting to accomplish in present-day China.

Visit to
a Village

When my husband, Nan, and I returned to mainland China for the first time in 1979, our visits to our families followed a distinct pattern: most of my relatives lived in urban China, whereas his tended to be scattered in rural areas. We shared a common bond with the ancient land. Both of our families had left the mainland for Taiwan in the late 1940s, and the search for our relatives was a joint venture throughout.

Tuxian village in Anhui was where my husband's mother and her family had come from. With no current address in hand, we had tried writing to the local officials asking for assistance in locating Nan's relatives but had received no response. As we traveled south from Beijing, where I had been reunited with my cousins, we took the chance of venturing into Tuxian on our own with no real expectation of making any connections there.

Thus decided, we set out on a sunny morning by train from Nanjing, hoping that the telegram we had sent the day before to the village officials would at least forewarn them of our arrival. From the train we watched the country-side as we went by, the more cultivated land and green earth of eastern China. A few hours later our train was pulling into the local train station when we saw an official car carrying the Red Flag emblem on the trunk—Red Flag was the brand name of those Shanghai-made automobiles —zooming through the front gate of the small station onto the platform and then past all the waiting passengers. We watched in astonishment as three officials stepped out of the car. They were waiting in line as we descended from the train. Introducing themselves as the welcoming party, they quickly ushered us into the waiting car and took us to the government guest house in town. We later learned that we had been given such an elaborate reception simply because relatively few visitors came from the outside—we were the second American couple to visit the village since the relaxation of Sino-American relations.

The car took us through the village center, a familiar scene in rural China: dirt roads, low residences built of concrete or bricks, some made from mud and rice straw. Livestock roamed the streets among the playing children who were bare-waisted in the summer heat, with slitted pants to facilitate their going to the toilet. They stared at our passing car and we returned their gaze with equal fascination.

We were accompanied by two deputies and one party secretary to whom we had written about the purpose of our visit. All three were eager to describe life in the village for us. It was a fishing village. There was no major industry except agriculture in the surrounding countryside. Yes, they had located some of Nan's relatives but most of them lived on a commune outside the village. Nan was elated about their finding his relatives and about being in the same village where his mother had grown up, although he was as much a stranger there as I was, having never set foot here before himself.

We were driven to the official guest house, next to the village headquarters, and shown to our quarters. It was a charming, turn-of-the-century room, complete with a rosewood bed under a white mosquito net hung from the high ceiling. In a corner stood a rosewood dressing table with a mirror that had seen better days. Under the bed was a washbasin, something I had not seen since my childhood. For a few minutes I was transported in time and space to Grandmother Li still presiding over the Li household in Wuhan, living in a similar room. Thirty years had gone by like a flash, leaving only these rare objects to evoke old memories.

Afternoon tea was served and pleasantries exchanged. Soon the village mayor came to join us for a cup of tea in the lounge adjacent to our bedroom. The charm of rural China will always be the simple, warm hospitality of its people. We were welcomed, in fact, as an extension of the village family, home for a visit. Whether we chose to take these expressions literally or not, it was difficult not to be moved by the warmth and sincerity of these people.

We talked about our relatives and the process of searching for them. The village office had located Nan's aunt, sister-in-law to Nan's mother, after tracking down her old address. Though she had since moved to a commune away from the village, it had not been too difficult to locate her given the household registration system of all citizens in China. Additional relatives had been found through her. It was decided that we should first visit the aunt out of deference to her senior status in the family and the close relationship between Nan's mother and the aunt's family, whose families had been neighbors in Sichuan during the Sino-Japanese War. Given the late hour of the day, we also agreed that an early morning departure for the commune would be more appropriate, especially in light of the distance.

With a few hours to ourselves, we enthusiastically accepted the offer to visit a few local points of interest. Comrade Song, a young, intelligent assistant to the party secretary, volunteered to take us around. Comrade Song had lived under the Nationalist government but remembered only the negative aspects of pre-Liberation China. He considered himself very "red"—very Communist—devoting his life to building the new China. As we explored the local historical ruins that afternoon, he pointed out the many improvements being planned to make the village a tourist attraction for the future.

"When will that be?" we asked him.

"Oh, perhaps in three to five years. You'll see." He was full of confidence. "And I hope you will return to check it out."

Comrade Song was correct on the urgent need to restore the few precious historical sites that had suffered substantial damage during the Cultural Revolution. We visited Ouyang Xiu's Drinker's Pavilion. Ouyang Xiu was a famous poet of the Song dynasty some nine hundred years ago. We were appalled to see the senseless destruction of his famous calligraphy on the rocks and tombs. The only untouched site was his manmade stream, shaped like a winding maze, down which he floated his drinking cup from one end to the other, cooling the drink in the process.

Another site we visited, the Langya Temple, had also been damaged. The Buddhist statues in the temple had been axed or smashed into pieces. The paint on the front door was faded and covered with anti-religious slogans scrawled by the Red Guards. Inside the temple the old monks had returned to their religious devotions, joined by a few young monks. Walking around the outside of the prayer hall we came upon a small mound of rocks behind the temple. Slender green tree sprouts were growing from cracks in the rocks, defying their harsh environment and reaching out to a new life.

Life had gradually returned to this temple. We sat in the adjacent tea room to take afternoon tea with the monks and exchange thoughts on the future of Buddhism in China. Slowly but surely, we felt, Buddhism would regain the vitality it had had before the anti-religious movement.

After a restful night we set out in the morning for Shahe, which means Sand River, where we would meet Nan's aunt and other relatives. Comrade Song came along with us and, during the long jeep ride, gave us more information about the commune. It was a small commune of 1,000 households, relying primarily on agricultural products, though in recent years there had been emerging interest in developing light industry on the commune. Bicycles and sewing machines were two products being considered by the commune leadership as potential new products. There was limited use of farm machinery. The commune still depended basically on manual labor to cultivate the land.

Mr. Song explained that we should be prepared for the natural curiosity of the commune residents, as they had not been visited by outsiders in recent years. Curiosity was a mild expression for what we encountered.

The commune residents were lining the streets as our jeep pulled in, leaving barely enough room for the jeep to pass. Faces smiling and inviting, the people clapped as we rode on as if we were visiting dignitaries. We waved at them, village residents and friends of our relatives, and at their children who will, one hopes, have more contact with the outside world.

We rode into the commune hospital compound, where we would meet Nan's aunt who had traveled four miles that day to meet us in her daughter's house, as her own was not accessible to automobiles. The compound was surrounded by brick walls, the hospital itself being the only concrete structure. The rest of the buildings, including the aunt's house, were made with the traditional materials: mud mixed with rice straw, dried to a yellowish tint.

Nan's aunt came to the door as we got out of the jeep. Standing in front of the low house, she looked tiny and frail, a petite woman of about sixty, in a navy blue shirt and pants. She beamed at us, smiling her toothless smile, and as Nan went over to hug her, she started to cry. The rest of the relatives who had gathered all started talking at once.

Once we were seated, I had the opportunity to look at the roomful of people. Dr. Ma, the aunt's son-in-law, was the host and the speaker for the group. Next to him stood his wife and two small children, a boy and a girl. Another couple with a small boy were standing to the side of the room, smiling shyly as they waited to be introduced. They were the aunt's farmer son and his family. In another corner was the aunt's unmarried daughter, still in school. The aunt's husband was in another province several hundred miles away, having been reassigned by the government during the Cultural Revolution to be "reformed."

Nan's aunt had married into an upper middle class family. Her husband was a practicing dentist when Liberation came to the village. During the anti-intellectual movement of the Cultural Revolution, he was removed from his profession and sent to a farm to be "educated." Nan's aunt had never quite recovered from the family disintegration that resulted from this forced separation. She and her children had been assigned to this commune farm, where they remained to this day. Her resentment toward the Cultural Revolution seemed to have been redirected toward her son who had left high school to become a farmer. As if he were a painful reminder of what the family had gone through, she seemed to blatantly disregard him, ignoring his presence in front of us. In contrast, she seemed to pay special attention to her son-in-law, Dr. Ma, who was the commune's herbal physician and who enjoyed a higher social standing. Nan's aunt was rather blunt about her criticism of the "peasant ways," criticizing the manners of her son and daughter-in-law, a woman who had a robust complexion and an awkward, shy demeanor.

Dr. Ma took charge by inquiring about our journey and our travel in other parts of China. More comfortable and at ease than the rest, he was the most articulate of the group.

Nan's aunt was now a bitter woman, openly critical of government policies. Her criticism at times caused embarrassing moments for Comrade Song, who stayed with us during the family reunion.

I sat and listened as Nan reminisced with his relatives. I was feeling somewhat sorry for the women in the room, as none of them dared to speak up. Once Nan's cousin, the unmarried daughter of his aunt, tried to make a point and was quickly dismissed by the aunt. I had always known that women in rural China did not enjoy much status in the family. Being in the same room, I now saw the real picture with my own eyes.

We left in the late afternoon after a festive banquet put on by the commune leaders. Nan would later return a few more times to Tuxian. After each visit he would bring back news about his aunt and her family.

The last time he went his aunt had moved back to the village with her husband, who had been allowed to return at last. What surprised me most was the news about Dr. Ma: the aunt's daughter had divorced him on grounds of wife abuse. I would not have surmised, based on the brief visit to the commune, that serious problems existed between them.

China is changing, and village life is part of the change. Somehow I was reassured by the decision of Nan's aunt's daughter. Her divorce indicated that rural Chinese women were beginning to stand up for their rights.

18

Those Managerial Women Of China

I did not seek them out. They had been there all along, quietly contributing their talent and energy to Chinese society. They seemed to have a no-nonsense air about them. Most had worked their way up from the ranks. Most had been closely connected with the Communist movement in China, and some had participated in the historic long march to Yenan. They were the managerial women of China.

Examining the statistics, it was clear that they had accomplished much in three short decades. Chinese women represented about 21 percent of the delegates to the National Peoples' Congress. Fourteen of them were governors or lieutenant governors of various provinces, fourteen were deputy or assistant secretaries of national government ministries, one was a cabinet member, and three were on the National Peoples' Political Consultative Council.

I did not set out to study Chinese managerial women during my initial trip to China. I was too involved in absorbing the changes in China and reuniting with my lost relatives to pay much systematic attention to women's issues. Yet, no matter where I went, I noticed them. They were everywhere, in every walk of life, and by sheer numbers, they demanded recognition. Gradually, I found myself speaking to them individually, either as part of my getting to know the agency they represented or in their roles as women managers. I started filing away impressions I formed about them, the insights they had shared with me, and their place in modern China. Ms. Li, the head of an embroidery factory near Beijing, was one example.

I was visiting my cousin Zhenli in Beijing at the time. After seeing a number of historic spots and universities, I expressed an interest in visiting a typical factory, having learned that systematic reform was beginning in the factory setting to create the competitive edge China needed in production and management. Zhenli got one of her friends to arrange a visit to the embroidery factory the next day.

The factory was located on the outskirts of Beijing, across the city moat, now a shallow winding river surrounding the Imperial City. Standing by the factory's front gate waiting for our arrival was the head of the factory, Ms. Li, a slim woman of medium height, in her fifties. She was wearing a white cotton shirt over a pair of gray pants with the shirttail hanging out over the pants. She was totally at ease as she came over to shake our hands and escort us to the briefing room to begin the tour.

The room was on the second floor of what seemed to be an administration building. Awards and certificates adorned the walls. As if on cue, Ms. Li gave us a comprehensive presentation on the factory organization, its production, and the projected goals for the year. Two male deputies, about her age, sat quietly next to her waiting for her to complete the orientation.

After asking a few factual questions about the factory I turned to a subject that had intrigued me since meeting her at the gate. I asked if she had been the head of the factory for very long.

"Just over two years," she replied.

I asked if her predecessor was also a woman. She said no, and added, "But the choice of me was logical enough. When you consider the fact that 60 percent of my work force are women, it is quite logical to appoint a woman as the head of the factory."

I smiled. Yes, it was logical enough, but not so simple, even in the more liberated West. I asked why the appointment of a woman was only recently made.

Ms. Li laughed good-naturedly. She looked around at her male deputies and said, "You are right that it took us a long time to come to this decision, but we had to start somewhere."

Ms. Li had devoted much of her energy during these short two years to creating a more humane work environment. The daycare center for the female employees' children had been expanded and renovated. For those who brought lunch to work, a special cooking facility had been set up for warming the workers' lunches. An award system had been established for each production unit, using a point system to reinforce worker incentive and provide a foundation for the special bonuses awarded at the end of each month. As I toured the factory with her, she seemed thoroughly familiar with the operation of the place and stopped frequently to chat with her staff, who had been her co-workers for more that twenty years.

I would meet a few more women managers like Ms. Li on my subsequent trips to other provinces. In Tianjin, for instance, I had the occasion to visit a special school for deaf children. There again, the principal was a woman, a former teacher in the school, who had recently been elected principal of the school, for her leadership and demonstrated competence.

It was not unusual to have managers nominated from the staff, particularly in the educational system. The only woman president of a leading university, Dr. Xide Xie, had been elected by her faculty to head Fudan University in Shanghai. Prior to her appointment to the post, she had been an active researcher, professor of physics, and one of the vice presidents of the university. Dr. Xie explained to me when she visited Albany in 1987 to receive an honorary degree from the State University of New York at Albany, that all major universities in China used a similar selection process for naming the university presidents. I wondered whether this in part explained the scarcity of women holding college president positions, as the majority of all university faculties were men.

There was little doubt that the "old boy network" was alive and well in China. The recent change of guard on the national level did not produce any woman political leaders. Many older leaders had retired from active politics, but they were all replaced by younger males, with not a single woman in sight even for future promotion to the top leadership. The relatively few women who occupied important posts on the National Political Consultative Council have all retired and left the political scene.

I remember Ms. Yang, the former vice minister of the Ministry of Health, and chair of the Chinese National Red Cross Association. Ms. Yang retired in 1985 and was replaced by a man. Yet when I first met her in 1979, she had seemed full of hope for a bright future for the women in China.

I first met Ms. Yang at a banquet held at the Beijing Hotel. Ms. Yang had given the banquet for us, having taken pains to offer Muslim cuisine in appreciation of my ethnic background. When she walked in the door I saw a short, stocky woman full of energy and vitality, looking much younger than her seventy years.

Ms. Yang had joined the Communist Party at an early age and had followed the Communist leaders in the Long March. Single and unattached, she devoted her full energy to her work. She was candid about her choice of not having a family: "I would not have been able to devote myself to my career if I had tried to raise a family," she said. "I have compensated by getting involved in health and welfare issues for all families." Indeed, as the chair of the National Red Cross Association, she had enough projects to keep her busy in addition to assuming the full-time role of vice minister of the Ministry of Health. Ms. Yang expressed a personal interest in my family, including my parents in Taiwan and my brothers, one of whom she had met while he was on a scientific exchange program in China as a visiting professor of physics. She seemed to make a special point of offering her personal services for any request I might have. Over a toast of maotai, she said, "I'd love to have you as a friend, if you don't think I am too old for it." We drank the maotai and vowed to see each other again on my next visit.

I have exchanged letters with Ms. Yang since then. I looked her up on my 1985 visit to Beijing but she was out of town of business. I learned that the same year she had stepped down from her post at the Ministry of Health and retained only a consultant role with her other associations. I thought about her wish to see more women in politics. I wondered what she was doing about it now that she had finally finished her own work.

Another memorable woman, Lei Jieqiong, Deputy Mayor of Beijing, could also trace her connection to the early revolutionary days of the Chinese Communist movement. I met Lei on my 1982 trip to Beijing, during a short stay at Beijing University where my husband and I were guest speakers in the Department of Sociology. As was typical when entertaining overseas visitors to the university, we were given a banquet at a restaurant near where we were staying. The university car took us to a popular place to eat, close to the campus, one frequented by both locals and outside visitors. As we stepped out of the car we saw that another car had just pulled in. Out stepped a tall, neatly dressed silver-haired lady with an unusual flair. I was introduced to Deputy Mayor Lei.

Lei was in her late seventies but moved like a woman decades younger. She had on a light blue nylon shirt over a pair of light gray cotton pants. A pair of white leather shoes were her only compromise to "extravagant" comfort. Most Chinese in 1982 still wore plastic sandals.

Once seated, I learned of Lei's other connections with the university. She was in fact an adjunct professor of sociology, having earned a master's degree in sociology, in the early 1930s from the University of Southern California. She returned to China upon completion of her graduate degree to join the Communist movement.

Lei came from a prominent Mandarin family. Her father had been a leading newspaper editor and a practicing attorney who had been an advocate of equal status for Chinese women. Lei was one of the few women of her generation to receive a higher education abroad who participated in the early Communist movement that strongly advocated the equal status of women. Mao's teaching that "women hold up half of the sky" was a basic dictum of Chinese Communist doctrine. Like Yang, Lei decided early in her career not to have any children, and although she married, she remained childless. Instead, she devoted her whole effort to her multiple careers. She continued to be active in the academic community after her retirement from the post of deputy mayor in 1985.

Watching and listening to Lei was a rare treat. She was perceptive and sharp. At the dinner table she spoke of the effort underway to provide better diagnosis of mentally retarded children, and we had a lengthy conversation about the pros and cons of using existing screening instruments available in the West. Lei was mindful of not repeating the same mistakes as the West, including the long struggle to mainstream handicapped children.

Both Ms. Yang and Ms. Lei have retired from active service, and apparently no female leaders have followed in their footsteps. Perhaps in time China will have a new generation of women managers and leaders. Without ties to the revolutionary past, the new Chinese women managers must compete from a different foundation. Without the traditional family structure to support them, the new Chinese women managers must rely on their own resources.

In the more open society and increased contacts with the West of recent years, China is being subjected to Western influences. Unfortunately not all Western practices have been conducive to improving the status of women. The return of the importance of physical appearance has reinforced the old feudal perception of women as sex objects rather than equal partners in the workplace.

A nursing home director, a young woman in her early thirties, put this dilemma most succinctly during my visit to her nursing home: "I knew I was offered the job because most men did not want to be a nursing home director, but I'm going to prove that I can turn this into a dynamic place, that only women can run it properly."

She had joined the Communist party at an early age, doing public relations work for the Red Army. This job offer was a result of her tenacity and hard work and her long hours of self-study. With limited formal education and training, she was studying gerontology in her spare time. Like most younger women managers in China, she no longer wanted to forgo motherhood, and fortunately for her, her husband was supportive in sharing the child care responsibilities.

As we toured the nursing home together, she would stop to hug or kiss an elderly man or woman, full of encouragement and compassion. One woman who had recently reached the enviable age of 102, beckoned her from a distance; she was shy about meeting visitors head-on. As the director turned to go over, she commented, "We are all women, from the same big family of womanhood."

I watched her walk proudly over to the elderly resident, and smiled. I knew she meant for us to keep our faith and our unified front in our joint quest for a better future for women, in China and everywhere else.

The Men of New China

I met them first as my relatives—some I had not seen for more than thirty years, some I had never met before my return to China in 1979. Then there were the officials I came in contact with, strangers I met on the street, professionals I became acquainted with during my tours of universities and human service programs.

They were the men of the new China. Like men elsewhere, they defy stereotyping. Yet they could not completely escape generalization. They share a common thread as Chinese men; common traits that demand recognition from an outsider, particularly from a Chinese women coming home from abroad.

My first point of contact with my male relatives took place in Wuhan, central China, my mother's home province, during my 1979 trip to search for lost relatives. In Wuhan I met my fifth aunt's second husband.

Fifth Uncle was a small man in his sixties with an authoritative air. He spoke slowly and deliberately, head tilted back, eyes looking down at the listener. As the third or fourth ranking official in the Wuhan Provincial Government, in charge of the import and export business, he enjoyed certain privileges including a better housing allowance and a substantially higher salary than most others,

Having met my fifth aunt's first husband long before, I found myself comparing the two men. The current fifth uncle somehow did not reassure me that my aunt had not made another mistake in marriage. Her first husband had previously married a rural woman, a fact well hidden from fifth aunt until it was too late. While bigamy was illegal, neither my fifth aunt nor the other wife ever pursued legal recourse. Instead, my aunt grew away from her police chief husband until his imprisonment in 1949. She met her present husband in the same provincial government where she had been working as an accountant. The marriage was his first and her second.

In Wuhan we stayed with my aunt's family in their apartment. My fifth uncle assumed the role of host and ushered us into the family living room. There I witnessed the traditional male Chinese host at work, something I had seen again and again since childhood. While he started the conversation, the women of the house scurried in and out of the kitchen serving tea and refreshments. He was served tea first, before the guests and he alone directed the flow of the conversation.

Fifth Uncle soon relaxed and his discussion shifted from official rhetoric on the virtues of socialism and communism in China to more personal inquiries. He wanted to know our employment status, salary level, and those of our relatives abroad. While such questions were not considered in poor taste by Chinese standards, as they are often intended to express one's interest and concern for the visitor, it became apparent that my fifth uncle obviously had other purposes in mind. He began to drop a few hints about his wish for a color TV set. We had already brought a tape recorder as a gift. A transistor radio I had brought on the trip for personal use caught his attention He asked if he could have it as well. I gave it to him, noticing the embarrassment on my fifth aunt's face. Yet she said nothing.

As I was anxious to speak to my fifth aunt, who had a close relationship with my mother, I found my fifth uncle's domination of the conversation trying. Seeing no intervention from my fifth aunt, I took her cue and did not pursue my own inquiry into the family until the next day when we had some time together alone. Now that she had the opportunity to do so, Fifth Aunt explained that she was reasonably content with her second husband. Despite his gruff manners he remained loyal and faithful to her, something she could not say for her first husband.

Not all the male relatives I met that summer in Wuhan were like my fifth uncle. Jia, husband of my cousin Mingqiong, and a journalist in his fifties offered some glimmer of hope for Chinese males. Jia had had a long career in journalism, covering social and economic issues for a local newspaper. He had met Mingqiong while both were working near the North Korea border during the Korean War. Mingqiong was then a member of a recreational troupe and Jia a young journalism student. Two daughters came from this marriage and, unlike most Chinese fathers, Jia clearly devoted himself to them despite their female gender. Jia was especially attentive to Mingqiong, who had suffered an injury during the Korean War that had resulted in a dislocated hip bone. He would take her arm crossing the street—an unusually tender gesture for a Chinese husband—and helped her push her bicycle in and out of buildings. My husband, who had had an earlier career in journalism, took a liking to Jia immediately and the two of them soon disappeared into a separate room to compare notes on their experiences.

In Beijing I would meet my other male relatives, my cousin Zhenli's husband, Chi, and my own cousin Ma, son of my second aunt.

I had clear memories of my second uncle, who used to bellow at the maid, Spring Flower, in their Wuhan house where I visited occasionally. I had an image of my cousin Ma as a clone of his tyrannical father. I couldn't have been more wrong.

Cousin Ma was now married to a musician. He himself had become a composer of ethnic music and held a teaching post at the local college. My visit to his house and family, with one young daughter, surprised me. He was the chef, cleaner, and entertainer for the evening. His wife told me that she rarely cooked the meals, since Cousin Ma was a better cook and had effortlessly assumed the major household responsibilities. Cousin Ma would laugh at the distant memories of his own father and the time when the women had little say in the division of labor at home. "Well, this was part of my marriage contract from the beginning," he said. "And the Cultural Revolution made it necessary for me to be more than half a parent when my wife and I were separated by our job assignments for several years." During the time they were working in different cities, when many couples had to undergo prolonged separation as part of the government policy to punish the privileged class, Cousin Ma also took care of their infant daughter. He assured me that he was not exceptional, that many men of his generation had also become more flexible about role reversal at home. His wife said rather emphatically, "Male chauvinism is now frowned upon in China."

Cousin Zhenli's husband, Chi, was another example of male acceptance of what traditionally had been considered "women's work." Born and raised in northern China where traditional male dominance prevails to this day, he was not only supportive of Zhenli's career development in the Ministry of Education, but he himself had continued to advance to bureau chief in the national news agency while assuming the role of primary house-keeper at home. Like my cousin Ma, he came from a family in which women had historically held low status. Indeed, whenever Zhenli visited his family back in their rural community in northern China, she was reminded of how insignificant the women were still considered: the womenfolk had to sit and eat separately. Yet Chi had broken with tradition to accept his new role in his own home. His rationale was simple and pragmatic: Zhenli's frail health would have made it difficult for her to assume any heavy household burdens. "The work had to be done, whether by a man or a woman is irrelevant." he commented.

Zhenli and I discussed this emerging trend in China. Zhenli explained that equality for women in the new China has been government policy. It was getting easier for men to assist women at home, given the national push for women to enter the work force. Unlike some of their American counterparts, she argued, the Chinese woman worked because she had to, not because she wanted to. By contrast, Zhenli noted the difference in how the overseas Chinese men approach their role at home. In many ways the traditional values had been preserved more strongly in the overseas Chinese communities than on the mainland.

In 1987 Zhenli finally had the opportunity to visit me in the United States. She was intrigued to find out that despite my "liberated views" on life, I continued to carry out the traditional responsibilities of a Chinese woman at home, and that many American women continue to assume more than half the work load at home. She was rather scandalized to find, in a nation known for its support of women's rights, that the reality did not match the rhetoric. She became concerned that Western influences, if allowed to permeate Chinese society, might have an adverse effect on the hard-won position Chinese women had acquired. She had good reason to worry.

A few months after she returned to China she wrote to express her alarm at the consumption of beauty products and fashionable clothes by Chinese women. "It appears that Chinese women are turning into sex objects, the very image they had tried to shake off many decades ago. Chinese husbands now want beautiful wives who can perform as hostesses while holding down a good job. Are we going backward?"

The male willingness to accept responsibilities at home was still largely an urban phenomenon in China. When I met my cousin Lianfeng again in 1982 in Chengdu, I had a glimpse of the relationship between rural men and women. Wife abuse was common and a typical female response to the male's dominance was sadly desperate and potentially fatal, evidenced by suicide attempts. The wife of Lianfeng's step-son had tried to kill herself several times after arguments with her husband.

The one-child family planning policy also had a profound impact on the role of women in China. There was an increasing number of unexplained infant fatalities and abandoned handicapped infants. During my 1985 visit to the Children's Welfare Institution near Guangdong I visited the nursery where disabled infants had been left in hospitals, unclaimed. The majority of them were infant girls who would not survive beyond infancy.

Not too long ago a visiting woman sociologist from Shanghai shared with me her views on the future status of women in China. Also concerned that the position of women in China might be heading backwards, she maintained that women were as responsible as men for the implementation of the one-child family planning policy. "Remember, women have joined men in agreeing that a male child is far more desirable," she said.

"You may be right, but who has conditioned the women to think this way?' I asked. We both sighed.

One striking feature continued to impress me about Chinese men: their total loyalty to their family and children. What binds men to their families has been their need for unquestioned support and the need to offer their own support to members of their clan. Most of the Chinese men I have gotten to know during my recent trips to China have devoted substantial time and energy to building a better future for their children and grandchildren.

It will probably take several more generations for Chinese men to fully accept the equal role women must play in Chinese society. As China opens its doors to the outside world it must also respond to outside influences including the more permissive, individual choices made by men and women in the West. For more than thirty years, China has relied on official pronouncements to achieve equality for women. Today it must rely on persuasion and individual choice. The road to women's equality will be long and arduous.

I shall continue to hope for a better future for Chinese

women, and for their men. My hope was at least encouraged one afternoon in 1982 at the Wuhan Technological University where I had just completed a series of lectures.

I was walking out of the classroom accompanied by an old gentleman, a professor of philosophy from another university, who happened to be in the audience that afternoon. He mentioned a book he was reading, Marilyn French's *Women's Room*, in which he had noticed a deep and pervasive anger among women toward men.

"I felt I could understand the rage of women in the book," he said, "for I could think back to my own mother's tormented life in the old feudal China." He spoke softly, looking ahead down the long, shady campus road.

The summer dusk had begun to set in, deepened by the shadows of the trees along the road. He conveyed more than his acknowledgement of the book. He shared with me his own understanding of the Chinese women's struggle, past and present.

As I listened, I thought how far we had come, two generations apart, to have a conversation like this on a subject that had been taboo in the old China and was not an easy subject even today. I felt a sense of gratitude for this moment of truth, a fleeting encounter with another human spirit, a male Chinese, a thousand miles from home and thousands of years from the feudal past.

Part Four

WOMANHOOD—
THE UNIVERSAL BOND

CHAPTER

20

My Asian Sisters

On my way to an afternoon movie in town, I accompanied my friend Pearl to get some money from her father who was a physical education teacher at the middle school. After searching through the school buildings, we found her father in the faculty lounge in a tight embrace with a female student a few years our senior. They looked startled as we walked in on them. Pearl was so upset by the scene that she fled the room, leaving me at the door dumbfounded. I followed Pearl back to her house. She had retreated to her own room, her dark mood unchanged. I sat down, but could find nothing to say. I knew this was not the first time Pearl had caught her father in the arms of another female. The secret I shared with my adolescent girlfriend cast a long shadow over us. I could hear Pearl's mother singing a sad Japanese folk song in the backyard as she hung out the clothes to dry.

I realized even then, as an eighth grader, that Chinese and Japanese women shared one thing in common: they accepted their husband's philandering as stoically as they accepted their own destiny in life. Pearl's mother was Japanese. She had married a Taiwanese during the Japanese occupation of the island.

It has been said that Chinese men have three wishes in life: a Japanese wife, a Western style house, and Chinese food. To Chinese men, a Japanese woman was the ideal male fantasy—soft, yielding, and selfless.

I have also known another image of Asian women. My grandfather's concubine, the woman who eloped with his lieutenant, was a high-strung Burmese woman with a cunning, indomitable spirit that is also Asian. This type of woman would not tolerate for long any position that made her inferior or subservient to men.

In her autobiography, *Facing Two Ways*, Shidzue Ishimoto, the famous modern Japanese feminist, has described her own struggle in coming to terms with her independence from men. Her husband, who had exposed her to the more liberated Western thinking and had helped her search for self-identity, withdrew his support when her behavior became "less Japanese."

After his long and hard effort to put spirit into a doll-like creature, and just as his labor began to bear fruit—that is to say, just as I learned to express myself, my husband said to me one day that he thought my appearance was losing charm for him. . . . Now he frankly declared that the beauty of a Japanese woman lay only in her naivete. He pointed to the delicate feminine figures in the old prints, pronouncing them his ideal. He reverted to the "good old" ways of his people marked by masculine hauteur. The "inferior sex" could stick to its grace and modesty. He would not lift another finger to change habits and customs.[3]

During the New York State delegation trip to Japan, I spoke to a couple of modern Japanese feminists about their current struggle. One woman writer was openly sarcastic about the slow pace men were taking to recognize the equal status of women in Japan.

"Do you realize men don't even know where their underwear is in the house?"

Our female delegation members were scandalized by her statement and probed for more details. She remained adamant that men were helpless around the house and apparently preferred to keep it that way, to further the assumption of household responsibilities by women.

Yet we found on this tour that there was a pending crisis for Japanese men as well. As more men retire at an earlier age, they find little or no role in their own home, having abdicated all household responsibilities to women a long time ago.

For the Japanese women, the reform movement actually started in the nineteenth century. During the Meiji period (1868–1911), Japanese women were influenced by the progressive movement in the West. Their efforts focused however on the more general social welfare, rather than on the specific improvement of the status of women, as the Tokyo Women's Reform Society stated in its bylaws in 1888:

> The purpose of the society is to develop the dignity of the women by reforming corrupt social practices, cultivating morality and prohibiting drinking and smoking.[4]

The Japanese women who joined the early women's movement tended to be teachers or former teachers, influenced by Western religious teaching.[5] However, the improvement of women's status at work was largely due to the working women and their involvement in the labor unions of the early twentieth century. Japanese women began to vote in 1945, at the end of World War II, under the American occupation, about three decades later than Chinese women.

Ironically, it was the Japanese protectionist movement, which at the turn of the century won better working conditions for women, that is now contributing to the slow progress of women in the work place. By making women special at work, the movement inadvertently hinders the acceptance of women as equals.

During my 1985 visit to Japan, our delegation was headed by a woman, with three other women and five men as delegation members. No matter where we went, we were greeted by an all-male cast, the only exception being the interpreter for the group.

At one of the welcoming luncheons, the women in our group began to ask rather pointed questions about the role of women in government and business. The issue of hiring more women into managerial positions came up. "Do you believe in recruiting more women into higher managerial positions?" I asked the official host. A brief silence followed. I had broken the code of the demure Oriental woman.

"Yes," the answer came somewhat reluctantly, "I personally have no problem with it, but it is difficult to implement." Indeed an elusive answer to a hard question.

Our interpreter was bemused by this exchange. Later that evening, as she joined our group for supper, she spoke of her own chosen profession. She explained that it was commonplace for Japanese women to be foreign language interpreters. Given the limited employment options for female college graduates, many women gravitated toward the job of free-lance interpreter because of its flexibility and access to the men's world.

"Do you honestly think that I could have sat in the same room today if I were not the interpreter?" She asked rhetorically.

Young unmarried women are under far greater restrictions in life than their male counterparts. When we visited South Korea, my husband and I had one evening out with a group of college students from Yongsei University, drinking and talking in a favorite college pub. In a more relaxed environment, the students soon forgot about the passing time. All of a sudden a female student jumped out of her chair exclaiming, "My goodness! I'm late for home. My parents will be mad at me!" I looked at my watch. It was only nine-thirty. I asked her, "Do you have a set time to go back home?" She explained that all unmarried women had to follow curfew hours, some self-imposed, some imposed by the family.

In India, the women's movement had been shaped by influences from the West, especially from England. The Indian Women's Association was formed in 1917 with the primary mission of improving welfare for women, children, and the poor. The women leaders, professional women from higher socioeconomic classes, followed a path similar to that of their other Asian sisters, with one exception. From the outset, the Indian women's movement leaders had sought to enhance the special status of women, not merely obtain equal status.

Indian women found their homegrown supporter in Gandhi, who had freed them to participate in the national movement with him. Gandhi believed in equality between the sexes:

> Woman is the companion of man, gifted with equal mental capacities. She has the right to participate in the minutest details of the activities of man, and has the same right to freedom and liberty as he . . . By sheer force of a vicious custom, even the most ignorant and worthless men have been enjoying a superiority over women which they do not deserve and ought not to have.[6]

At the University of Michigan I met a few professional women from India, dedicated to women's causes. Compared to other Asian women, the Indian women were more aware of the need to enter the political arena.

Unfortunately, all women's movements in Asia seem to have suffered from a soft strategy and a lack of connection with the masses they represent—their approach is generally educational and conciliatory. Their tactic is one of quiet acceptance, and they tend to be led by women who have not suffered much themselves.

In Hong Kong, something exciting has occurred in the women's movement. Influenced more by England than by the traditions of China, Hong Kong women have emerged as a strong force to be reckoned with, many of them entrepreneurs and corporate leaders in the business world.

A friend of mine who was in the same doctoral program at Columbia University with me is now a successful businesswomen in Hong Kong. In addition to her teaching post, she now owns an import-export business, and a private consulting firm. A member of an old well-to-do Hong Kong family that left the mainland before the Communist takeover, she enjoyed a higher standard of living throughout her education in Hong Kong and abroad. When I last visited her in 1985, she had launched a personal research project into the child rearing practice of China's one-child planning policy.

We went to Victoria Peak one evening to get a better view of the Hong Kong harbor. It was a magnificent summer night, and the harbor lights, viewed from the top of the mountain, were truly magical.

I asked her about her next goal in life. She avoided answering me directly.

"You remember asking me the same question when we were at Columbia?" she asked me. I said yes. She had indicated back then that her only wish was to teach college.

"Look what you have been able to accomplish in such a short span of years," I commented.

She smiled in acknowledgement. She was not one of those modest Oriental women; she took the compliment easily.

"Time has changed for women in Hong Kong. I am taking every opportunity that comes my way. However," she turned more serious, "I am still single. You pay a price for what you want."

I thought about the meaning of her words. For many Asian women, even American women, the road to success is never without its personal and emotional price. I knew my friend might have chosen singlehood in any event, having never expressed an interest in men to my knowledge, but her point applied to more than a few women interested in advancing themselves in the world.

"With all that," she said, sensing my mood, "I would not have done anything different."

Indeed not.

21

An American Friend

The early spring morning air on the Virginia Farm came through my bedroom window. I tugged at the quilted blanket Nancy had put over me before she went to bed herself. Reluctantly, I opened my eyes to this small guest room. Next to the door hung a childhood photo of Nancy, a young ballerina trying out a pair of dancing shoes. She had the same sweet smile, a bit sardonic, even at that young age. I first met Nancy when we were both working at the Henry Phipps Psychiatric Clinic of Johns Hopkins Hospital in Baltimore.

I got out of bed to find Nancy already up, preparing a sumptuous breakfast in the kitchen. Her cat cuddled next to her feet, she turned to greet me, "You slept well? You city folks don't appreciate the country morning." She looked out her window at the spacious meadow. "I usually get up at the crack of dawn. It's a very different routine for me now."

Very different indeed, I thought, as I remembered the fun-loving, fashion-conscious Nancy I had known. The woman standing here had given up the trivialities of life. Yet her sense of herself seemed stronger than ever.

I had gotten married in 1966 after completing my master's degree in social work at the University of Michigan. Following my husband to his new position in the Social Relations Department of Johns Hopkins University, I had landed a job at the Hospital, working as an inpatient psychiatric social worker at the Phipps Clinic.

On my first day at work, Addie, the Director of Social Services, who had met me that year at a conference in Chicago and offered me the position, took me on a grand tour of the hospital. In the psychiatric outpatient clinic I met Nancy for the first time.

Sitting behind an old walnut desk was a petite, pretty young woman. She had the thickest Southern accent I had ever heard.

"How are you? Welcome to Phipps." She got out of her chair to greet me.

Addie left us to talk. In a few moments, Nancy managed to shatter all my preconceived notions about the ultra-feminine Southern belle—she was the most assertive, openly aggressive, and utterly charming Southern woman I had ever met.

Nancy came to the point, wasting no time in small talk. Treating me as if I had been her friend for years, she outlined for me the dynamics of the social service department at Johns Hopkins—young, newly trained social workers joined by other equally dynamic new graduates in nursing and psychiatry, were quickly challenging the old-line establishment, creating a sharply divided ideological line between them. She went on to describe in great detail the personalities involved, pointing out things I should watch out for. She concluded, "Remember, you are a woman, and this is a male-dominated institution."

Her "you are a woman" brought me closer to realizing what I shared with other women. As the only Asian woman on the professional staff, it was natural and logical for me to identify with these other women, Caucasian and black; I began viewing myself as a member of a different minority than Chinese.

As soon as I returned to my new office, the phone rang and it was Nancy arranging for a lunch date. Thus began our long, close association.

As a teaching hospital, Johns Hopkins was fertile ground for new experiments in psychiatric intervention in the 1960s. The Therapeutic Community Model, first started in England by Maxwell Jones, was being implemented at Phipps in full force. To promote a more people-oriented therapeutic milieu, all staff had shed their uniforms and attended daily community meetings. New roles and old roles were being sorted out; the consulting psychiatrists were available to help deal with the staff's adjustment to this new model of behavior. New programs in behavior modification, psycho-linguistic technologies, family therapy, the human potential movement, were pursued side by side with the more traditional psychoanalytic and psychodynamic approaches. Over time, Nancy and I each developed our special interests, Nancy in crisis intervention, I in family therapy.

We had close contact with other professional staff members at Johns Hopkins, as well as with paraprofessionals and citizens trained to be members of the treatment teams. The suicidology program turned out many fine professionals whose initial training had been in other fields. The mental health counselors were housewives trained in counseling techniques. All in all, it was an exciting time for us.

Against the backdrop of this stimulating environment, my friendship with Nancy blossomed. An English linguist who was part of the sex research team at Phipps and a psychiatric nurse working in the emergency room sometimes joined us for lunch. It was a time for swapping the latest from the hospital rumor mill or for some serious debate on the status of interdisciplinary teams in a hospital setting. Thrown into the company of non-Asian women, I was becoming more aware of the similarities and differences between Chinese and American women.

For example, it was rather startling for me to find that American women could be as reluctant as Chinese women to upset the male order of things, and would go out of their way to acquiesce to men. American women in general paid more attention to maintaining a youthful appearance. Open communication with men in their personal lives was as difficult for American women as for my Chinese women friends. And our English friend would relate in great detail her own trouble in openly disagreeing with her husband over minor incidents. Such difficulty also extended to the older women I got to know at work. One Black social worker, single and getting on in years, expressed her own frustration at the attitude of men friends who took her for granted. I was equally struck by the desperation of the younger women, some of them in their late twenties, who were deathly afraid of getting old and losing their physical attraction. Even Nancy, with all of her rhetoric about female independence, could not escape the same behavior patterns adopted by other women when relating to men.

However, the women's underlying resentment toward men for their dominance over women was always present.

Our lunch conversations usually turned to gripes about the male staff at work. I found that I had the fewest grudges against the men, simply because of my lack of experience in the States. I had had a different life in a different culture. My frustration over the treatment of Chinese women had not been transferred to the new environment—I could not be angry at a white male establishment that had had little part in the oppression of Chinese women in China. I was still too unfamiliar with the plight of American women, or the Chinese-American women in the States, to connect my destiny with theirs.

Cultural differences were more exposed in an intense work setting such as Phipps where the emotions of the professional staff were subjected to close scrutiny as part of the training and therapeutic process. I soon discovered another fundamental difference between the East and the West in coping with mental stress.

The psychodynamic school of psychiatry emphasized the developmental framework of mental illness, and the treatment strategies underscored the expression of pain and anger in order to develop better coping mechanisms. Here was a new phenomenon for me—anger. Not that Chinese women do not get angry, but the anger is usually filtered down and expressed in more indirect and subtle ways, which according to the Western theoretical framework could be labelled "passive aggressive" or "passive dependent." Open expression of one's anger, particularly for a woman, was alien to the Chinese. After sitting through dozens of community meetings, group sessions, training conferences, and seminars, I finally learned to say "I'm angry at you" with some ease and conviction. Nancy kidded me about my "confrontation" technique, a routine therapeutic technique in working with the mentally ill.

"When you confront someone," she would say, "you make it sound like, Confucius says. . . ."

I had my response ready: "That's because I have combined two therapeutic principles, confrontation and acceptance. I can confront and make it sound like gospel truth at the same time."

But I drew the line at abandoning the traditional role of Chinese homemaker when at home. Nancy found it hard to understand how an assertive professional, as I seemed to be at work, could turn into a willing, compliant homemaker with such relative ease. She was particularly puzzled by my lack of resentment toward the additional responsibilities my immediate and extended families often created.

Once my sister-in-law, as a young graduate student, came to visit with a dozen friends of hers; they all stayed for dinner. When Nancy heard of this, she was outraged. "The nerve of her! Without consulting you in advance!" It was difficult for her to understand that I took these cultural expectations for granted, and I rarely questioned them from a Western perspective. I continued to fulfill these obligations, even as my work outside the home became more demanding, simply because it was easier to complete the tasks—with more efficient time management on my part—than to fight against them. I must confess I saw these demands as more a challenge than a burden.

Yet on a personal level, I was grateful for Nancy's moral support. Her anger on my behalf was especially important, showing her care and concern. In return, I offered the same moral support to her during her difficult romance with a physician friend, and during the aftermath of their breakup.

Nancy and I had different recollections of how this relationship ended. I recalled Nancy telling me how she finally came to the determination that their relationship had to end. She was cooking supper in the kitchen. When she came out to the living room, she found her friend dozing off on the sofa; a performance repeated each time they got together. This time something snapped inside her. "Who needs this?" She said to herself, and made up her mind to get out of it then and there.

Nancy thought I had given her too much credit for coming to her senses. "Actually, the darn thing lasted far too long and died a slow death," she said. She added, "I was so afraid of being alone then, but no more."

Nancy came from a prominent Virginia family, her father a physician, her mother a nurse. Nancy apparently broke with her tradition when she left Virginia to pursue higher education up North, to get a graduate degree from Smith College. Most of her childhood girl friends had settled down in her home community after high school. As the eldest child in her family, Nancy naturally assumed a nurturing role toward her brother and sister, both of whom had troubled marriages. Nancy, for a variety of reasons, chose to remain single.

Nancy celebrated her thirtieth birthday on a trip to San Francisco with my husband and me. I was expecting our first child then, and Nancy walked through Golden Gate Park with me, letting me rest every mile or so. We visited the famous Haight-Ashbury district, appalled at the wasted young lives hanging in the doorways, half-stoned, with flowers in their hair, but with no energy for living. Walking the streets of Chinatown with Nancy made me realize some of the acculturation I had undergone. I was now equally comfortable in both worlds.

Two years after I first met Nancy, she was offered the opportunity to direct the training program for a Suicide Prevention program in Buffalo, New York. I went up to visit her. We ended up working overnight that weekend in her crisis center, handling the hotline and talking elderly women out of attempting suicide. Nancy was her happy, productive self.

Then we both became preoccupied with our individual lives—I moved on to the Department of Child Psychiatry at Shepperd and Pratt in Towson, Maryland, and later to the New York State government, while Nancy left New York to return to Virginia. She was managing a mental health facility while teaching at a local college. I made arrangements to visit her but had to cancel the trip for personal reasons.

It was only a few years ago that I picked up the thread of our friendship again. Meanwhile, I had heard that Nancy had become disenchanted with city life and wanted to return to the farm where her sister's family lived. Nancy became the loving aunt to her niece and nephew. She settled in a small community nearby, working at a local hospital. The glories of higher positions seemed less important than the peace and satisfaction she had found for herself.

I have visited Nancy a few times on the farm. On one of my recent visits, we took a walk after supper along the country dirt road. The fragrance of honeysuckle filled the air. It was a quiet walk, each thinking her own thoughts.

We had just had another debate on the subject of men and women. Nancy was insistent that men were useless in this world. "Look what they have done to civilization. It's completely messed up," she said. "I believe the conflict between the sexes is irreconcilable. The war will go on forever."

"But the fact is that we are still living together on this planet," I suggested. "Don't we have a responsibility to live in peace?"

Nancy was set on her theory that the white male establishment would not give up its supremacy in the name of equal opportunity without some fundamental revolutionary change. Being white and Southern, she deeply resented how women in the South have been treated, their opinions ignored.

"What is the solution then?" I asked. "It's not to hide or drop out, but to gain an active voice in the affairs of the world."

The evening shadows began to lengthen, and Nancy was silent for a while, before finally replying.

"You know, I agree we should be more actively involved. I still contribute to women's causes—even though I have not been active on my career goals for quite some time now."

I could again smell the rich fragrance of the honeysuckle by the roadside. The summer air was getting heavier and darker, summoning the mystery of dusk. For me, the world could always be better, and the riddle of man and woman would always dominate our consciousness.

In deference to our more than two decades of friendship, I was content at that moment to remain silent.

Notes

1. Han Suyin, *Birdless Summer,* New York: Bantam Books, Inc., 1972, p. 26.
2. Sax Rohmer, *The Insidious Dr. Fu-Manchu,* (New York: Pyramid Books, 1913), pp. 27–28.
3. Baroness Shidzue Ishimoto, *Facing Two Ways: The Story of My Life* (Stanford, California: Stanford University Press, 1984), pp. 298–299.
4. Sharon L. Siever, *Flowers in Salt: The Beginnings of Feminist Consciousness in Modern Japan* (Stanford, California: Stanford University Press, 1983), p. 87.
5. *Ibid.,* p. 89.
6. M. K. Gandhi, *Young India,* No. 26, February, 1918. p. 270.